RISING ABOVE

RISING ABOVE

A GREEN BERET'S STORY OF CHILDHOOD TRAUMA AND ULTIMATE HEALING

SEAN J. ROGERS

HOUNDSTOOTH
PRESS

RISING ABOVE

A Green Beret's Story of Childhood Trauma and Ultimate Healing

ISBN 978-1-5445-1844-2 *Hardcover*

978-1-5445-1843-5 *Paperback*

978-1-5445-1842-8 *Ebook*

G. Baker

This book is dedicated to my grandfather Gerald Baker who joined the United States Air Force when he was sixteen and served in the Korean War. When he was getting out of the military, he took a standard job aptitude test as part of his out-processing procedure. The test said he would make a good mechanic. So my grandfather told me he had just assumed the test knew something he didn't and opened a forklift repair shop, which he ran successfully for over fifty years. He showed me through his actions how to be a man, how to respect people and take care of your family before all. It would take years of working through my trauma before I was able live a life that resembled his, but he has always been my guiding light. He is my North Star helping me navigate the trials and tribulations of being a man. Even though he has passed, I seek his guidance every day by remembering the man he was.

CONTENTS

PREFACE

BEFORE I START DOWN THIS PATH AND RETURN TO THE deserts of Phelan, California, I must say a few things. Outside of my immediate family, there aren't many people who have heard these stories. They cut deep, and some family members are still struggling to make sense of how they affected their own stories. Despite the possibility of these memories drumming up old pain for those who have yet to face them, they have the potential to reach other people who have had similar experiences.

If we fail to use our pain and struggles to grow and help others, then we experienced them for nothing. Our minds are our greatest asset, and no matter how trapped you may feel in your current circumstances, your mind can never be imprisoned. You will always have the power to think, and thought produces action if utilized correctly.

INTRODUCTION

—

WHEN I FOUND MY WIFE NAKED IN BED WITH ANOTHER man, it was like a vase shattered before my eyes. I knew that no matter what I did, that vase would never be the same, and no amount of glue could put it back together. No matter how badly I wanted to go back, I was stuck in this new reality that I did not want to live in. It was a blur of anger, sadness, and pain. I was twenty-one years old and about to have my world turned upside down.

I saw a game loaded in my PlayStation that I had never played. The nerve of this man to load a game and entertain himself with my PlayStation and my wife! So, while this man cowered in the corner of my bed, covering himself with my blankets, I punched the TV into the wall. While I put my fist through the screen, I seethed over a glass handle of vodka sitting on the table and thought, "You cheap bastard." Then I picked up the vodka and threw it at his head.

My wife started to dial 911, and I knew I had a decision to make. I could hurt this man in ways I could only imagine or leave now and avoid a life sentence. I opted to leave, and as I drove, I screamed into my steering wheel, hoping it would wake me up from the nightmare.

I drove home to the desert of California; my childhood home was my only option. I drove one hundred miles an hour the entire way. The speed served two purposes: for me to crash and wake up to a different reality, or for the cops to stop me and save me from myself. I made it to my brother's house and went to bed pretending that this was all a bad dream.

The next few days were some of the toughest of my life. I cried, I drank, and I slept. For the first time in my life, I didn't want to be me anymore, and it was a difficult thought to have in my head. Two days into my grief, I had a realization that would change my life forever—my entire perspective and approach to trauma would never be the same again. It was the single most pro-found thought I have ever had. I stopped feeling sorry for myself and asked myself a very pointed question: "How can I win this?" I sat on the couch and realized I was losing control over my best asset, my mind. Then it came to me: she cheated on the man that I *was*, and I didn't want to be that man anymore. I wanted to be a man she could never obtain again—someone who was far too good for her. I was accepting the loss of my old reality and ready to build a new one. Instantly, I felt powerful again. I felt like my future was back in my hands; I had a purpose, and I was ready to grow.

I wish I could say from that point on, things started looking up. But there was one major issue with my new plan: my past. I had to go back and face it in order to move forward.

I didn't realize it at the time, but my past was not only my greatest obstacle; it was also the key to my success, and without this realization, life would have not changed for me. Like many others, I would have committed to change for a brief moment only to quickly resort back to my old habits. This behavior was so predictable for me that it was sickening. I would get motivated, take steps toward change, then do something completely stupid and fuck it all up. It seemed no matter what I did, it was only a matter of time before the old me took over and ruined everything. I was thirty-three before I finally figured out how to stop the cycle of stupidity.

I began journaling and digging into my past to break this cycle. I found the key to change, and this book is not a result of the process—it *is* the process. There was a dragon within me burning down every opportunity in front of me, and I spent my entire life failing to get away from it. Until finally, I realized it needed to be tamed. Now my dragon burns down obstacles and clears paths for opportunities. I ride that dragon like Daenerys Targaryen, the Dragon Queen from *Game of Thrones*, and I have never been so free.

But in order to tame the dragon, I had to go back.

AERIAL ASSAULT

—

ONE OF MY FIRST MEMORIES IS OF WHEN I WAS A SMALL
boy, and my mother, a single mom, had recently gotten
a new job. She dropped us off at a babysitter's house
before she went to work. I had never met this sitter
before, but my brother and I were instantly excited
when we arrived at her place. It was a farm! There
were animals everywhere and we couldn't wait to play
with them.

My mom talked to the sitter for a few minutes while
we waited for her to come back and let us out of the
car. My mother introduced us, and the sitter seemed
like a nice lady. Within minutes, she shooed us off to go
play. I was certain I'd spend the rest of the day running
around outside until my mom came back.

Thirty seconds into our awesome new adventure, I found myself face-to-face with something evil. Neither of us moved a muscle, and it stared at me with hatred in its eyes. It looked like a chicken, but it was twice the size of one, and it was mean with its chest puffed out. It let out a terrible war cry and came at me with every intention of tearing me to pieces. I stood there frozen in fear, knowing the pending assault would not end well for me.

I was about three feet tall at the time and I was eye to eye with this thing. As it gained ground, its wings expanded and flapped with all its might, winding up for an aerial attack. The next thing I knew, it was airborne, clawing at my chest and flapping its wings in my face. It was a horrific assault.

Finally, the sitter calmly walked over and shooed that son of a bitch rooster away. I could tell she had been laughing, and I was pissed. I spent the rest of the day inside the house trying to figure out how I would get from the house to the car without coming in contact with that stupid bird again. Despite the evil rooster attack, this is one of my fondest memories—it's the last time I remember my mother being responsible and working.

Returning to good times is an essential part of this journey, and when I was a boy getting chased by a rooster, I had no stress. I didn't feel like I was going without. I felt fulfilled, and without realizing it, it was one of the last times I would be free to be a child without stress and anxiety constantly lurking around me. I have no doubt that if this stress-free path had continued, I'd be a different man today. Unfortunately, that path was over.

Soon after the rooster attack, I remember my brother and me sitting in the back seat of my mother's car speeding down desert roads. I had my knees on the seat and was facing backward out of the rear window. A man in another vehicle was chasing us. I had no idea what was happening. I watched in amazement as he reached out of the window while speeding down the bumpy dirt road and pointed a gun at us firing two rounds. One of the rounds split the top of our car's roof right down the center. The other hit the emblem on the trunk of the car and deflected downward. If it wasn't for that emblem, that round would have went into the center of my chest. That was how our new reality was shaping up, and it all began after the accident.

THE ACCIDENT

—

WE WERE AT MY GRANDPARENTS' HOUSE IN ONTARIO, California. They owned a forklift repair company, and the house was connected to the shop. When my grandparents were working, all we had to do was walk next door to see them. They were highly respected, and that place was a safe haven for us. It was my favorite place to be as a kid.

I'll never forget the day my mother needed to run some errands and asked me to go with her. I told her I'd rather not go because I wanted to keep playing with my new toy motorcycle, but my mother insisted she didn't want to go without me. Feeling needed and important won me over, so I strapped in. The next thing I remember is being in the hospital.

For me, that accident was just a blip on the radar. For my mother, it was the beginning of the end. She soon fell victim to the opioid epidemic, and it didn't take long for her to become a full-fledged addict. She manipulated providers into filling her scripts despite the obvious signs of addiction, and she got kicked out of doctor's offices. Somewhere along the way, my mother also became bitter. Everyone was against her and the world owed her something. As I sit and write and think of all she had gone through, I feel less angry with her—I'm sad. She did awful things and made poor choices, but she also endured truly difficult circumstances I would never wish upon anyone. I have no doubt she felt like she had to endure those things in order to protect us.

Somewhere along my mother's path, she met a man named Steve, and we moved in with him almost immediately. He had two sons about the same age as my brother and me. We hated them, and they hated us. My sister stayed out of the feud, but between the boys, it was war. We gained their father's acceptance, something they so desperately longed for, and we saw them as weak and annoying. We fought them often and not in the way kids usually fight.

I remember when one of the brothers, Shane, who was my age, talked bad about my mom. In response, I pinned him to the ground and grabbed a handful of his hair, then I slammed his head into the ground until the hair let loose. He was left with a fist-sized bald spot on the top of his head. It was always my brother and I versus them, and we were not about to lose.

Shortly after moving into Steve's place, my mom stopped leaving her bed. Months had gone by, and she hadn't been up. She was in a constant slumber, and we kept waiting for her to come back. Finally, I broke down and asked Steve if my mom was going to die. I was sobbing when he hugged me in a cold, disconnected way, and he whispered that she would be fine. Then he stood up and walked away as though I was never there. Little did I know, Steve was the one causing it all. He kept my mom in a drug-induced coma to collect her income checks. Steve knew my mother was going to leave him and decided he couldn't let that happen. I spent months thinking my mother was on her deathbed because of this guy. I would like to say there is forgiveness in my heart, but if I saw him today, there would be an ass whooping.

DARK DAYS

—

THESE MOMENTS WERE SO PAINFUL AND SHOCKING FOR me as a child that I began to disconnect from people. I felt so alone. This is where things got tough for my older brother, Chris, as well. Between the ages of eight and ten, I needed him as a protector. I depended on him for physical and emotional support, and this was a lot for a boy to take on. And he wasn't protecting us from school bullies—he was protecting us from grown-ass men who beat us like we were adults. My sister's father was especially violent toward my brother and me. He would break spoons on our backs and throw us around like rag dolls. Every time one man left, another replaced him. When they moved on, it was a relief followed by anxiety and fear. It felt good to watch them go, but we knew the next one might be worse. Looking back, it must have been more obvious to those around us than we thought—Child Protective Services was at our house regularly.

Chris adopted the role of protector and spent his childhood defending my sister and me. I see now that this role was too difficult for a boy, and it didn't translate well into adulthood. Once my sister and I no longer needed his protection, he found others who did. He became the protector of people whom he felt he could save. This noble way of life brought him down into their problems and created more issues than he could handle alone. To this day, he struggles with his anger and need to nurture in his heart. He struggles to know who he is and what his purpose is.

Chris taught me that you can't help others if you have neglected yourself. Even if you are trying to help others to *fix yourself*, it will not work—you have to face your own past and examine it. Determine what effects it had on you. Why did it hurt so badly, and how does it affect you to this day? Road rage? Inability to trust in relationships? I am sure the negative effects come to mind without effort.

This is only the start; you cannot accept the bad without the good. For all of the things I struggle with today,

I accept that those things are equally responsible for my successes.

A BRIEF BUT BRIGHT MOMENT

—

AFTER WHAT SEEMED LIKE AN ETERNITY, MY MOTHER finally moved out of Steve's house, and my grandparents moved us into a mobile home they owned in the desert. There were no boyfriends and no other kids to contend with there, and things were good. My mother was still addicted to pills, and this pill addiction drained her soul. She was a shell of her former self, but at least she came out of her room and let us know she was alive. It was like the drug Soma from *Brave New World*—she took the pills to forget and to not feel pain.

One powerful memory was the time my mother spent all her money on pills. She even sold her food stamps for them, too. We had no food, and she was too high to realize the severity of the situation. She asked a friend of hers, an elderly woman who lived down the street, for help. The lady told her she had nothing except for four giant bags of frozen French fries that someone had given to her. My mother called me into her room where she normally spent twenty hours a day in bed, and said, "Seano, these fries are all we have for the next couple of weeks until I get paid again."

That hurt me.

It hurt because I knew she had put herself and the pills first and that I was on my own. That was the day my mind started to change, and the resiliency in me started to grow. I knew I could no longer rely on my mother to provide, and I had to start thinking about how to take care of myself. I started to accept the loss of my old reality and started focusing on the new one. I decided not to dwell on the fact that ten minutes prior to this moment, I didn't have to worry about eating. That reality no longer existed.

I took on my new responsibility and learned how to make fries in every way imaginable. I baked them, pan-fried them, microwaved them (not my preferred method), and ate them with salt, ketchup, or mayonnaise. I had a mission to survive on these fries for two weeks, and nobody could know. If anyone found out, Child Protective Services would be at our house again. This time, they would find an empty fridge, and we would be taken away for sure. Those two weeks with the fries were the beginning of a new understanding: Mom's not coming out of this. I had held my breath for years, hoping my mom would kick this addiction and no longer need those pills. My siblings and I had held on to an old reality. We held on to how Mom used to be, hoping she would one day return to us. Little did we know, things were about to get a lot worse.

As I went through my past seeking answers to who I am and how I got here, the incident with the fries was instrumental. Those two weeks were the key to everything I have achieved. If I could walk into that kitchen and talk to that boy baking fries, I would look him in the eyes and tell him to get ready. He'd need to suck it up and embrace the pain that was to follow. I would tell him to avoid self-pity; there would be no remorse along his path. He must learn to get hard and look out for himself. Most importantly, I would tell him that he would be broken, and the sooner he stopped running from that truth, the sooner he would become his own man.

This is the essence of this book: Learn the cycle of trauma so you can quickly overcome it. Then accept that your traumas have shaped both the good and bad qualities of your life. But merely accepting this fact is not enough—without *understanding* those qualities and where they come from, you will never learn how to use them. You will find yourself in situations and wonder how you got there. You'll wonder how you allowed yourself to get to that place.

You might want to blame your circumstances, but it's likely you had a lot more to do with shaping your circumstances than you would ever like to admit. Emotions like anger, frustration, cynicism, pessimism, you name it, can all be signs of un-nurtured trauma. Once you allow yourself to become the victim, you will never own them; they will always be at the helm of your ship. You'll always be sitting on the deck hoping to survive the storm. There is no worse feeling in life than lacking control over your own destination—feeling as though it is your circumstances, and not you, that control your outcome.

THE RANCH HOUSE

—

SOME OF THE BETTER TIMES OF MY LIFE OCCURRED WHILE living in the ranch house. The "ranch house" is what we called a singlewide trailer that was on my grandparents' property in the small town of Phelan, California. It was a small mobile home, but my grandparents always made sure we had a roof over our heads. My grandparents had bought five acres of land in the middle of the desert to start a ranch. My grandparents lived in Ontario, California, full time and worked their forklift company in order to provide for their kids, and the ranch was a place they could use to get away from the city life and the business in Ontario. They put three mobile homes on the land, and all of the homes ended up being filled by their children.

My grandparents were not fond of the revolving door of men in and out of their home in Phelan, but my mother could care less. The distance gave my mother enough freedom to do what she pleased with their property. There was one man in particular who used to come around every now and then. His name was Joe and he'd take my mom out on dates. Or so we thought. This guy never wanted anything to do with us. He'd come over and grab my mom, and they'd be gone for hours, if not for the entire night. My brother and I always tried to talk to Joe and constantly asked if we could go with them on their dates. They always brushed us off.

One morning, we woke up and realized Joe was still at the house. He had been coming around for a while, and our young minds mistook that consistency for a relationship. We wanted to get to know him, but no matter how much we knocked, Joe and my mom would not come to the door.

Now, when your mother consistently locks you out of the house, you learn the necessary skill of breaking into locked doors, and I successfully opened the door with a butter knife. Both of them screamed for me to leave. The next day, we came home and the door was completely different. Joe had replaced the old door with one made of solid wood, and it had a large dead bolt on it. He even replaced the doorframe with heavy-duty lumber—the door wouldn't have budged for a battering ram. The new door was their way of telling us they had no interest in us. They didn't want to get to know us; we were a bother to them and that door was going to keep us out.

Years later, my brother and I suspected Joe had been paying for my mom's company. It all made sense, and once it clicked, it made me sick to my stomach.

There were other instances when my brother and I thought we finally had a male role model around to guide us, only to be smacked in the face with the reality of their intentions. For example, one day my mom decided to put us in karate classes despite the fact we had no money. *Three Ninjas* was my favorite movie growing up, so I thought karate classes were the best thing ever.

One night, my mother told us our married karate instructor was coming over to discuss our performance. My brother and I waited eagerly by our bedroom door to hear how our ninja skills were advancing. We decided to peek around the corner, and we saw our instructor making out with our mom. It was as though she was incapable of attracting a decent human being, and every person in her life had some ulterior motive.

As a boy, I desperately sought approval from a man, and without a father or positive male role model to guide me, I felt lost and insecure about my growth. Looking back on the constant neglect, I see that the trend would never leave me. I'd always be seeking confirmation from others, and I'd desperately chase approval from those I admired. The fear of letting down someone I respected was a weight heavier than anything I could imagine, yet this desire to prove myself would also be the key to my success.

Going back through my past with an open mind and open heart revealed more traumas than I ever thought existed. However, with a little reflection, it is easy to see how the trauma shaped the strongest and most dominant aspects of my being. Without it, I'd be a weak and docile creature, too afraid to move.

Going back and reliving these situations was vital to my growth later in life. Reliving them allowed me to come to terms with who I am and why. Only when you know who and what you are will you stop seeking approval from other people. If you don't face your trauma, you will fail to acknowledge the power it bestowed upon you. If you go through life feeling powerless, you will inevitably resort to playing the victim, constantly allowing the opinions and actions of others to persuade you. You'll be weakened by your unwillingness to face your past and to own it.

OUR NEW "NORMAL"

—

NORMALCY AND CONSISTENCY WERE TWO THINGS THAT never lasted long in our household. Nothing jars a child more than continually evolving shit scenarios. Children are resilient and they naturally adapt to overcome the toughest of circumstances. Unfortunately, when there is never any consistency with good or bad, it's difficult to adapt. The constantly changing environment wreaks havoc on the child's soul. All I wanted was to feel secure, yet every new boyfriend brought new challenges and a new set of fears and trials.

I learned to disconnect and start looking out for myself. This was a key lesson because with nobody to rely on, I had to rid myself of excuses. If I was going to fail, it would be my fault, and the unfortunate reality of that truth taught me to manipulate my environment. People became pawns that needed to be moved around to accommodate my goals and desires. Relationships became superficial means to an end. I became increasingly sensitive to the feelings of others in order to read them and avoid getting my heart broken. I always wanted to know when people were growing tired of me so I could be the first to leave. I could not handle any more neglect and did everything to avoid it. I was an emotional wreck, learning to bypass emotional connection at all cost.

Just when I thought a bad situation was over, it would start all over again. First, it was a guy keeping my mother in a drug-induced coma, then it was a guy paying for her attention, then another, and another. Every triumph over these pieces of shit only landed us stuck with another one. Then my mom met a man named John, and things really got difficult.

When my mother met John, she was a full-blown addict with two major car accidents under her belt. (I was in the car both times, but I can't remember either one; I just remember waking up in the hospital.) She was selling herself for money and leaving us without food to support her addiction. Just in case she wasn't close enough to being a complete disaster on her own, she had to bring John into the picture, who was trying to cope with much of his own trauma from the past.

John was on his way home from work one night and saw a car wrecked into a tree. Smoke was coming from the car and he could smell the fluids burning. The accident had just happened and he was going to help. He checked the driver's side door and he could see a lady slumped over the steering wheel. She looked dead, but he couldn't tell, so he pulled her back and immediately recognized her lifeless body. It was his sister.

John's preferred reality was broken. It shattered in front of his eyes, and he didn't want it to be true. He went home, grabbed his shotgun, put it in his mouth, and reached for the trigger. The barrel was too long and slipped out of his mouth. He blew his left bicep clean off. Years later, he is a full-blown alcoholic who has yet to face his trauma, drinking every minute he is awake to mask the pain. Add a drug-addicted girlfriend and three kids into the picture, and the rest is history.

Things were awesome at first. John loved to cook and was super proud of his new trailer he had on a small piece of land. We went to his house to hang out, watch movies, and eat. It felt like we were moving up in society for once. John drove a newer vehicle and had a nice house. It felt good to be dropped off at the bus stop in a respectable vehicle. When you spend your childhood trying to hide how poor you are, these things matter.

One day, my mother and John had gotten into an argument. My mother was trashed and getting ready to jump into her car to speed away from his house. I ran up and tried to get into the back seat so I didn't have to walk home. As I opened the door, she sped off, almost running me over. I walked home.

As I got closer to our house, I noticed the car looked a little off, like it was sitting crooked. As I walked up to it, I saw the rear passenger door I had tried to get into was smashed all the way to the other seat. She had taken a corner too fast and slammed into a telephone pole. If I had gotten into that seat, I would have been killed. To make the situation worse, the damn car still ran. So from then on, if she drove me anywhere, it was in an old shit brown Cadillac with the rear smashed in. This thing *screamed* white trash.

I realize now that I have spent a good part of my life

running from that image. I hated being on welfare more than anything. I hated that my mom did not work; I hated standing in line at the grocery store paying for food with food stamps. I hated washing my shoes for the first day of school instead of getting new ones. I hated the sinking feeling in the pit of my stomach every time I came home. So when I left my house every day, I lived a lie.

It became so natural to lie. I lied about everything, and I said I went on trips with my family. I lied and said my mother was on disability from an accident; she was not on welfare. I lied about every aspect of my personal life until I started getting caught in my lies and I realized I was making my situation worse.

Until recently, I spent my life trying to accomplish things that would distance me from the poor white trash kid from Phelan. I thought of things that people thought were impressive and I did them in order to change my imaginary status. People from normal upbringings went to school, so I got an associate's degree, then a bachelor's degree, and eventually a master's degree. I thought people who came from normal upbringings do things like run marathons, so without training, I "ran" a marathon in the Czech Republic while stationed in Germany. I sought out medals for competing in Brazilian Jiu-Jitsu; I took seminars and classes to obtain certificates, diplomas, and awards. I was on a mission to be the person I always wished I was.

It took years of wasted effort and meaningless achievements to realize that running from myself was useless. This is the very reason why lottery winners are soon poor, why professional football players with multimillion-dollar contracts get arrested, why actors and actresses we all adore are depressed. We can add money and achievement to our lives, but it won't change who we are. You will still have the same issues you had when you were poor, and the same traumas will affect you. We can trade in the shit, brown, wrecked Cadillac for a Mercedes or a BMW, but it is only a matter of time before you do something that reminds you just how little you have changed. I believe this is because we all approach our history in the wrong way.

It took reflection upon years and years of different types of traumas to make me realize my past is powerful. The most powerful part of my history is that white trash kid from Phelan—the one I have spent nearly all of my life running from. That kid knows pain like most will never experience, but that kid also knows resiliency, humiliation, triumph, and defeat. That kid has so many life lessons wrapped up in thirteen years, and I am blessed to have him. He is a book that I need to read. He is untapped knowledge and strength that will be a source of inspiration for the rest of my days.

We all have our own version of a poor embarrassed kid inside of us. We all have things in our past we are ashamed of. We despise those experiences because they represent pain and suffering. However, instead of running from those things, we need to use them. Louis Zamperini, a World War II veteran and the inspiration behind the book and movie *Unbroken*, said, "One moment of pain is worth a lifetime of glory." Zamperini is telling us something here: he is telling us the most powerful moments we have are the ones that caused us the most pain. Yet most of us spend our lives running away from those moments.

When my mother left John's house drunk and slammed her car into the pole, it did not represent anything significant to me at the time. I was used to my mom being unpredictable and doing obnoxious things; however, she would always sober up and manipulate her way back into people's lives. It took less than twenty-four hours before it happened with John. Not only did they get back together, but we also moved into his house.

SUNDAY BARBECUES

———

I'LL NEVER FORGET HOW THE TRAUMA CYCLE STARTED AND became normalized in our household while we lived with John. It all started one Sunday with a barbecue. Music was playing, food was cooking, and it was off to an awesome start. My uncle came by and had some beers with my mother and John, everyone was in a good mood, and the *Best of Tom Petty* blared throughout the house. I thought, finally, something fun, something normal!

After my uncle left and the food was cold, my mother and John kept drinking, and before we knew it, they were in a full-blown argument over some trivial bullshit. I waited for it to end, but they were no match for each other. Neither one had an ounce of control, and neither one could stop the ongoing escalation. Soon, they were throwing plates at each other and flipping tables. It was as though they were in competition to see who could be more of a psychopath.

I ran to my room and locked the door. I sat on my bed, plugged my ears, and rocked back and forth praying. I prayed they would not turn their attention toward me. I was terrified. I kept hearing things smashing and breaking, and at some point, I finally fell asleep. I awoke the next morning panicked about what I was going to find when I left my room.

I walked out to broken glasses, plates and silverware flung everywhere, and an upside-down dining room table. But the important thing was that it was over. God had somehow lulled me asleep in the midst of all of that chaos.

Things were mostly calm throughout the week, with my mother usually passed out drunk before John returned home from work. However, the very next Sunday they had a barbecue. I thought, are they fucking kidding me? Do they not remember how the last one turned out? But they just pretended like nothing happened.

Tom Petty blared again, my uncle came over and left, and then shit started hitting the fan.

I'll never forget looking at my uncle's dog and being jealous of him. I thought, "You lucky bastard; you get to ignore all of this dumb behavior and just worry about yourself." That dog could care less how psycho any of these people were. As long as they dropped some food, he was good to go.

From that point on, coming home to that house caused a sinking, sickening feeling. Walking home and turning the corner to see that house produced an extreme amount of fear and anxiety. Anything could be going on in there, and I had no choice but to open the door and go inside. That was a horrible feeling as a child and a trauma that stuck with me forever. I was a prisoner in that house, and leaving it did not change anything. I found out the hard way a free person can be a prisoner. The fear of feeling stuck like that would never leave me.

One night, after another drunken Tom Petty barbecue, things took a darker turn. Of course, it started with plate throwing and arguing, but then my mom decided she was going to leave. John took her keys; my brother and I went into the laundry room to stop her because she was going to get in an accident. John handed the keys to my brother and told him to throw them outside. Chris threw them as far as he could, and my mother grew furious and tried to push past John. At that point, John shoved her hard, like she was a man. He shoved her into the wall with everything he had. I could tell instantly that the shove was not to push her away—it was to end this, and it was to end her.

My mom's head slammed off the wall with insane force, and she fell to the ground unconscious. John looked at her lying there and just walked out as if it were his plan all along. My brother and I started crying and panicking, begging her to wake up. We thought he had killed her until finally she started taking shallow breaths and slowly regained consciousness. My brother and I looked at each other, realizing things had changed drastically. We were no longer dealing with two drunk idiots—our mother was going to get killed. It didn't happen that night, but from that day forward, we knew it was only a matter of time.

The next incident took place not long after. As I walked home and turned the corner as usual, the sick feeling rose in my stomach once again. However, this time was different. I didn't need to open the door to see that things had gone south: my mother's car was part-way inside the house. The two front wheels were off the ground and the front bumper protruded into the living room. I started to panic. I knew that once John got home and saw this, he was going to kill her or all of us. This was not good and I needed to fix it.

I went inside and looked to my right, and sure enough, the front end of my mother's car was staring at me. I found my mother passed out in her bedroom. I woke her up and asked, "What the fuck did you do?" She looked at me, still drunk, and calmly said, "Took that corner a little tight," and went back to sleep. I couldn't believe it. She had no idea what she had just done and she could care less. It was as though she wanted to send John over the top, and she wanted him to just end her so she didn't have to deal with anything anymore.

I sat in that house for hours full of anxiety and panic waiting for John's car to pull into the driveway. I had no idea how far this was going to go. Then finally, I heard him pull in and my stomach sank and I got ready. I got ready to fight for my life and I was prepared to fight for my mother's. I took a deep breath as I heard the doorknob opening to the front door. I was ready for whatever I had to do. The door slowly opened and

I looked John right in the face, but he didn't look back. He stared blankly at the ground and walked right past me; I followed him to see if he was going after my mom. He got to his room where she was sleeping and I waited for him to launch his attack. But he crawled in bed and went to sleep. Part of me knew that this was a bad sign, but another part of me was so relieved that whatever was coming wouldn't be at that moment.

A couple of days went by with no response to the car still partially sitting in the house. Then, one afternoon I came home, and the front door was littered with bullet holes. I immediately thought someone was dead inside. I ran in and found my mother home alone. I asked her what the hell had happened. She said she and John started arguing about the car in the house. John went on a rampage about disrespecting his house and how nobody should disrespect his house but him. Then he grabbed his shotgun and a handful of shells, went out front, and started shooting rounds through the front door until he ran out.

These stories go on and on. I could talk about being chased through the house by John, and my brother coming out of nowhere to smash him in the face with a phone book to turn the attention away from me and on to him. Then he took a beating from the man at twelve years old. Or I could talk about leaving my crying sister locked in a room and telling her to stay hidden while I ran barefoot for miles through the dark desert to my aunt's house so she could save my sister from the fighting. Or the time I came home to a bullet hole in my bedroom wall that got lodged in my bookshelf, and my mom claiming she was "cleaning John's gun and it went off," when in reality she shot at him or vice versa. Or the nights when nothing bad happened, but we sat waiting for all hell to break loose. These moments were some of the worst of my life. Walking around with a constant knot in my stomach became overwhelmingly painful.

At some point, I realized there is always someone who has it worse than you. I met a couple of kids who lived in an abandoned house down the street from us. Their mother left them and never came back. My brother and I went to their house and watched them eat tortillas and beans out of the can. They were teenagers left to fend for themselves. They acted like they enjoyed the freedom, but we could see the pain in their eyes.

One day, we got our hands on some beer, and at age fourteen, it was my first time getting smashed. We were drinking at the abandoned house when an older dude showed up who must have been eighteen to twenty at the time. He kept talking about hooking up with girls, and I wanted to sound cool, so I talked about it, too. Later that night, I was getting sick from the alcohol and went to pass out on an air mattress in one of the rooms. That guy came in with a girl who looked eight months pregnant; I just pretended to be asleep. I could hear him telling her, "My little homie is going to smash." Then he started calling my name to have sex with this girl. I was terrified and wanted nothing to do with it, so I just pretended to sleep until he realized I wasn't going to wake up.

They had sex and passed out, and I saw my opportunity to get out. I could see my brother down the hall drinking a beer and I was trying to signal for him to come get me. I slowly got up and left the room, and my brother and I walked home.

In moments like these, you realize there are levels of abuse out there. When you think your situation is bad, you come face-to-face with a real-world catastrophe. These kids had no families and had nowhere to go. They were fucked and making life decisions they would never recover from. I hung on to these moments knowing my situation could always be worse. I knew that things were bad, but now I knew that they were not nearly as bad as they could be.

Finally, our time in the hell house came to an end. I am pretty sure John's family realized he was going to kill my mother and convinced him to kick us out. We packed up our stuff and went back to stay at my grandparents' ranch house. Unfortunately, once we got there, we found a giant pile of dirt about four feet high in front of the gated entrance. My aunt decided she didn't want us back on her parents' property, and she had my uncle use a tractor to make a huge pile of dirt to prevent anyone from driving in. This barely deterred my mother who backed up her eighties tuna boat Cadillac with the smashed-in rear door and punched it.

We shot up the mound hoping to clear it and then high centered. My mother couldn't care less; she went inside and told me to dig the car out. My aunt piled a half ton of dirt in front of the fence because she wanted my mother to stay away, but all she really did was create about four hours of work for me. I had to crawl under the car and pull dirt out with my hands. Covered in dirt and sweat, I finally got the car unstuck.

BECOMING THE PROBLEM

PEOPLE WONDER WHY KIDS HAVE TROUBLE STAYING ON the right path. Kids have a unique situation in that the victim mentality is real. They are actually victims. They are not allowed to leave; they are not allowed to better their circumstances by moving away or finding new parents. They are legitimately victims of their circumstances, which the law forces them to endure until they are eighteen.

While growing up, I always had better places to go and family members who took me in and tried to give me a better life. They tried their best, but then my mother would call the cops and they would come get me and take me back to her. It was like being told you had to suffer, you were chosen to endure a shitty childhood, and there is nothing you could do about it. Then, as adults, we look at these kids and wonder why they do drugs, fight, and get in trouble. The answer is because *they don't want to go home*. They are afraid of their homes—their homes are stress factories that make them feel like victims. The only control they have is to do what they want when they are free to roam.

Broken boys want to break things. It makes sense. If they are causing the pain, then they are not feeling the pain. Even if that relief is temporary, it is still relief, and young boys don't understand the difference between a brief moment and eternity. A brief moment of perceived power might as well be an eternity.

The only hope I had was turning eighteen and being allowed to make my own decisions. Unfortunately, I was only thirteen or fourteen years old; three to four more years in that life was far more time than I could bear. I was starting to lose hope; I found myself giving in to my impulses and becoming the problem.

I wanted to forget that tomorrow was coming—I wanted to embrace every ounce of right now that didn't hurt.

We hadn't been at my grandparents' ranch house for long before my grandfather purchased a different mobile home farther away. The house was purchased solely to give us a place to stay while keeping my mother at a distance. The new house was pretty deep in the middle of nowhere.

Shortly after moving in, we met the neighbors, two fatherless boys about our age who seemed to like getting into trouble about as much as we did. For a while, it worked out. We hung out with them and raised trouble around our new neighborhood together — until the day my friend told me his older brother was moving in to hide from a gang in Ontario. He said his brother was a gang member, and a rival gang had recently put out a hit on him, so he was moving to the desert to lay low for a while. I didn't pay much attention to it because my friend liked to exaggerate, plus I was only thirteen or fourteen and I could care less about gangs. Unfortunately, "Chad" we will call him, my friend's older brother, would come to wreak havoc on my brother and me. I had met Chad once or twice while hanging out at my friend's house. I could tell instantly that he was not someone to mess with. He constantly had gang bangers at his house drinking and acting like they owned the block.

One day, I was walking to my uncle's house, which was a few miles away down desert roads, when I heard a truck pull up behind me. I looked back and saw it was Chad, and I panicked because he was creeping up on me. I knew something was off or he would have sped past me without a second glance. I looked to my right and there was a chain link fence for another acre or so. I knew I wouldn't be able to outrun him in time.

He pulled up next to me and said, "Get in." I said, "I'm good, man. I'm just going to my uncle's." He pulled back a blanket sitting on the passenger seat, and I could see a gun. He said, "I'm not going to tell you again. Get in the truck."

I was terrified and knew something bad was about to happen.

He pulled up to his driveway, and I could see my mom standing in the front yard. I thought, "Thank God, she'll use all that crazy to help me this time." He told me to keep my head down. He said if I made a noise, he and his homies would shoot up my house with my mom and sister inside. He came around to the passenger door and pulled me out, then he took the blanket and covered me with it and guided me into his house.

Once inside, he took the blanket off, and there was a chair sitting in the middle of the living room. His two brothers were sitting on the couch, and he told me to sit down. Then he made a phone call, put it on speaker, and told the guy to let me know who I was fucking with.

The guy on the phone started spouting out all kinds of gang shit and told me he could have me green lit anytime he wanted. I could hear about five guys over the phone fighting to get on and tell me how fucked I was. I still had no idea what the hell was going on or why I was there. After about five minutes of gang members telling me how easy it would be to kill me, he hung up the phone. He pulled up a chair next to me and said everyone I loved was going to be shot for what I did. I told him I didn't know what he was talking about, and he finally told me I shot out the back window of his mom's house. Instantly, I knew what he was referring to.

His little brother found his gun and accidentally shot it off in the house and blamed me. Now this gang member thought I was shooting up his house. I thought, "Well, thanks, buddy; now, I'm dead." I kept sitting there thinking about how he was going kill me. Would he shoot me, strangle me, or bash my head in? Finally, he said, "If I ever hear…" Instantly, I latched on to those words. I don't even remember what he said after that. I knew right then he was going to let me go!

After berating me a little while longer, he put the blanket back over me and walked me to the truck. From there, he drove me about five miles in the wrong direction, and I walked back to my uncle's house like nothing happened. I kept that story to myself for years in fear of retaliation. I just kept thinking about how fucked up that situation was, how that kind of thing wasn't supposed to happen to kids. But I realized my situation was different and I needed to accept it and move on.

Things at home just seemed to get worse and they stayed that way, and the problem was that I was adapting to my environment. This was a survival technique for sure, and unfortunately, it was also the quickest way to outcast myself from society and become a person I despised. I spent more time with broken people to feel normal, and then I became even more like them. Then one day, I realized I was the one broken kids gravitated toward because my behavior was so bad.

I always knew deep in my heart that I was meant for more than getting arrested or joining a gang. I felt a pull at my heart to be better, to have higher expectations of myself. I just needed the right break to get away and change the course of my life. I knew that once that moment presented itself, I would be ready to take advantage of the opportunity and seize it. I knew in my heart that nothing was going to stop me. I was determined to take advantage of an opportunity that did not yet exist. Then, just like that, during one of my mom's drunken outbursts, she threatened to call my father like she had many times before and have him take me away. This was it. I told her to call him. I provoked her to get on the phone and make the call, and she did.

RUNNING AWAY, FOR GOOD

——

I MET MY FATHER FOR THE FIRST TIME WHEN I WAS FIFTEEN years old. He owned a restaurant in Fredonia, New York, and was an award-winning brewmaster. He came to visit us in California, then paid for my brother and me to visit him in Fredonia. It was a small college town full of beautiful old brick homes. Everything was rich and green, and I instantly loved the area. The atmosphere was different. People seemed friendly and didn't stare at you like they wanted to fight. We sat on the front porch, me age fifteen and my brother seventeen, smoking cigars and drinking whiskey. Clearly, he was unaware of how to be a father, but damn, this was the life!

I sat on that front porch and told him I was coming back for good. My brother said instantly, "Me, too, I'm coming back, too," but I knew he wouldn't. He was trapped by the life, he didn't want to break away from it, and he had become a part of it. Right then and there, I knew with 100 percent certainty that my brother would never leave that desert. He accepted that cycle as his destiny and made it his own.

That moment bothered me for years. I said with conviction what I was going to do, and I had every intention of making that happen. But my brother overshadowed the severity of my plan with empty words. The trip came to a quick end and we were on our way back to California, but things were not the same for me. I was focused and I had a plan. The opportunity I had been waiting for had finally presented itself and I was going to leave California for good.

I had obstacles to overcome, but I didn't think about those obstacles. I focused on the prize: I envisioned the end goal and allowed it to overcome me with joy and accomplishment. I thought hard and with great detail about how my new life would be, how I would improve my life with this new opportunity, and how to become a better person with better goals. I would leave the stress and anxiety in the desert and never look back.

This type of backward planning stuck with me forever. This "goal first, plan second" way of thinking aided all my future success. Until recently, I had never known where that way of thinking had come from, but as I dive deeper into my past, I know my childhood and the struggles I faced gave me powerful tools. From the day I decided to leave California, I never thought about how hard things were, and I never allowed myself to be overcome by the challenges of my goals—I simply ignored them.

I treated my goals like driving to a new destination. I decided where I wanted to go, and I visualized how beautiful that place was so I didn't lose motivation to get there. Then the most important part was understanding that someone had already been there. They already made the map from my location to the new destination. All I had to do is get the map and follow it. It was that simple.

However, this concept was lost on my brother, who always focused on the obstacles. He thought of a plan just enough to get excited; then he immediately dwelled on the obstacles that would get in his way. Those obstacles almost immediately diminished his excitement, and just as fast as it came, it was gone. This way of processing challenges is the greatest hindrance to success. You cannot succeed if you never try, and you will never try if you focus only on the obstacles you might have to face. It took me a long time to accept that you do not need all of the answers. You will figure it out along the way.

I knew I had an uphill battle when I got home to California. Despite my goal of wanting to live with my father, I still had the same challenges. My mother would just call the police and have me returned to her. I ignored that obstacle for the trip home, and I allowed myself to stay excited and settle into the idea of having a new start. I knew I would figure out how to make it work, and once the wheels of the airplane from New York landed in California, it was game time.

Coming back from New York was strange. My family expected horror stories about how bad my dad was. It was as though they were waiting for us to realize how good we had it in California. My family and I always had a strange relationship; I never felt part of their inner circle. My brother was, and I was able to see the difference between us. My grandmother loved him more than anyone, but this never upset me and never created conflict between my brother and me. I just knew I did not belong there with them.

The strange part was, I felt as though my entire family felt the same way. It was as though they knew I was different and they were waiting for me to leave.

When I returned home from that trip, I did not want my opportunity to be wasted. I needed to act quickly, but I also knew I had to be smart and not just up and leave. My mom would do anything to prevent her paycheck from walking out the door. She had physically restrained me on numerous occasions, once by sitting on my chest with her knees pinning my arms to the ground until I hyperventilated and had a panic attack. She would just sit there, watch me panic, and tell me to calm down. It was one of the worst feelings I have ever had, and I would suffer from claustrophobia for the rest of my life because of it. The hardest part was looking her in the eyes in the midst of a panic attack and seeing how calm she was. I begged for her to stop. She was breaking me, and I hoped that some maternal instinct would kick in and she would stop, but it never did. She watched me panic until I nearly passed out.

My mom had also hit us with broomsticks until she could pin us down and threaten to have the cops bring us home. Once, I used her own game against her when I tried to leave. She kept pushing me and grabbing the phone to call the police, so I punched myself in the face as hard as I could and started screaming for her to stop hitting me. She became pale as a ghost and looked at me like she had never done before. For the first time, she feared me. That stunt bought me a few days of freedom, but she eventually had me brought back. So if I was really going to leave this time, I needed to do it right.

I slowly started packing up my belongings and kept the luggage hidden. Each night, I packed a backpack or piece of luggage and hid it in a toy box, which I put inside the closet. Then I took the things I didn't want and threw them all over my room to make it look as though nothing had been picked up. I did this every night for about a week, packing my things and hiding them. I knew if she found my stuff packed and ready to go, it would be over.

I called my cousin, told her I planned to leave and needed a place to go. She said whenever I was ready she would pick me up and take me to my aunt's house.

Now I had to figure out what legal requirements were needed to make this work. My dad suggested I call the police department in New York and ask what they would need to not report me as a runaway. I called, and the officer informed me that a written and signed note giving custody to my father would be enough for them not to pursue me. I knew my mom would never sign a note like that, and at that moment, I felt defeated. But I had to try; I just had to be creative.

First, I tried cutting out the signature section and putting a school paper on top to trick her into signing the document. I filled out the document with the exact verbiage the officer said would be legally binding. I handed her the clipboard with the signature block cut out, and she immediately flipped the page. What is this? Damn…I messed up. She read the note and laughed, and then she threw it on the ground and said she wasn't signing it. I thought, well, plan B, which I had not thought of until that exact moment.

My mother was so used to being a manipulator for personal gain that she could barely recognize when *she* was being manipulated. I instigated an argument, telling her I wasn't going to leave until she signed the note. She started yelling and throwing shoes, then finally she got so mad she screamed, "Fine! I'll sign the note. It doesn't mean shit anyway!" I said thank you and immediately left the room.

Little did she know, obtaining her signature was one of the last phases of my plan. My belongings were already prepacked in my closet and my hideout location was set. All I needed to do was call my cousin for a late-night extraction, then call my father for a plane ticket. My cousin picked me up, and I was able to sneak out undetected with all my stuff.

She brought me to my aunt's house, and I called my father for a plane ticket. He answered, which was a relief, and said he would get online right then and there.

He called me back with good and bad news. The good news was he bought the plane ticket, and the bad news was my flight was three days out. I thought, shit, she's going to find me if I don't leave now. The entire plan depended on me being on a plane the same night or next morning.

The next day, while hiding out at my aunt's house, I received a phone call from my cousin. She said, "Your mom knows where you are. You need to leave now. I'll pick you up and you can stay at my place. She doesn't know where I live." I sat there waiting with my stomach turning, watching the driveway for my mom's big brown Cadillac to come screaming in. I had all my stuff in hand, and I knew two people were coming for me. My mom usually did seventy miles an hour everywhere she went, so I knew my escape was unlikely. Just then, I heard a vehicle screaming down the road. With my stomach in knots, I prepared for defeat and accepting this was just another failed attempt. I had run away so many times in the past and always got brought back, so this was nothing new.

I looked up expecting to see the shit brown Cadillac, but instead, it was my cousin! I welled with excitement and didn't even let her pull into the driveway before I started running toward her truck. I threw my stuff in the back and hunched low in case we passed my mother on the way out. Getting to my cousin's apartment felt like a huge step forward. I had the ticket, and now I had a hideout where my mom couldn't find me. I started to think I might actually get out of there.

A couple of days passed, and it was time to go. My cousin drove me to the airport, and I was gone. I made it happen and I felt so free. I gave my dad my word that

I was coming back and now it was all coming together. I tried to enjoy the experience, but I knew my mother too well. I knew this was not over, and if there was a loophole, she was going to find it. Having run away so many times, I had felt this excitement before. The excitement made the crushing blow of failure even worse, so I tried to ignore that my plan might have potentially worked.

By the time I made it to New York, my mother already found out I had left and immediately called the cops. As soon as I got off the plane, my father told me we had to go to the station because she had reported me as a runaway. My stomach sank again. I had come so far only to turn around and have to go back again.

I walked into the station with the note in my hand. I knew my mother was right and this handwritten note was not going to work. She was going to win again. This time was different, though—I was tired. I had put so much effort into this and I did not feel I had anything left. I had no more fight in me against this woman. I was going to head home with my tail between my legs and accept my circumstances. I couldn't keep fighting just to keep losing.

As we walked in, the officer was on the phone. I could

hear my mom yelling at him and I was standing four feet away. He was an older guy and seemed to be an experienced police officer. I could tell because he was barely phased by her berating, and he couldn't care less. He looked at me and said, "You have to go home, kid." Once again, my stomach dropped and I felt the all-too-familiar feeling of being trapped and alone. I told him I had a note my mother had signed, and while she was still yelling at him, he takes the note and reads it, ignoring her constant threats. He then cuts her off and asks her if she signed a note giving custody to my father. To my surprise, she says, "Yes, I signed that note, but it doesn't mean shit!" I looked at the officer waiting to see what he was going to do. He said, "Have a good day, ma'am," and hung up on her mid-sentence!

I was in shock. I couldn't believe what had just happened. My entire life, my mother had used the police as her pawns. She harassed them enough that they typically did what she asked to avoid the headache, but this cop was different. He couldn't care less how crazy she was, and he knew she wasn't getting into her car and driving to his station. He looked at me and said, "Have a nice life, kid," and handed me my note back. I stood there staring at him, deciding whether to hug him or start running. Just then, I felt my dad's hand on my shoulder nudging me to start walking. It was like God knew I was running out of fight and He wasn't going to put me through anymore.

This has been a trend throughout my life: God always knows the right time to intervene. He needs you to be tested for growth, so you have to suffer, but He knows your limits better than you and He's not going to let you stay down as long as you keep moving forward. From that moment on, I was a different person. I was no longer the victim of my circumstances. I made my plan; I made a decision to change my reality for the better, and I changed it. I would never again allow myself to be the victim that just took what was coming. I was different now; I had the control to change my fate. I was the writer of my destiny, and it was the best feeling I had ever felt up until that point.

When I look back on leaving California, it fills me with pride. I was given a mission that was seemingly impossible, and even at that young age, I knew I had to make it happen. I started to pull strength from that hardship and I could see it changing my behavior, something that happened so long ago I nearly forgot about it, yet here it was empowering me. Going back to that series of hardships, I realized the impact of every action I took. I was wasting my own life experiences by not acknowledging them for how impactful they truly were. These moments were building a dragon within me— one that I spent most of my life believing was a curse.

NEW LIFE, NEW EXPECTATIONS

——

THE FIRST COUPLE OF WEEKS LIVING WITH MY DAD, HOW-ever, I had to learn a new lesson. I remember telling my stepmom and my dad that I would be home by nine o'clock in the evening to finish my homework, but I had other plans. I was going to a party and I'd come home whenever I decided. That was the life I was used to living. I did what I wanted, when I wanted, and frankly, nobody gave a damn. Until now, I could come home at two o'clock in the morning completely hammered and it didn't matter.

This time, my father answered the door when I tried to sneak back in. He had a different look about him; it was a seriousness I had never seen before. The anger and intensity in his face was eerily familiar. I had seen those eyes before, with all that frustration and contempt. In his eyes was the same fire that burned in my brother and me. I had finally met my match, someone with the same anger and aggression. However, my dad had the size and strength to go along with it.

He started toward me, and I knew things were going south. I backpedaled through the kitchen and into the living room with him in fresh pursuit. I backed up into a reclining chair and waited to see how bad this was going to get. When he got to me, it was like fighting my brother all over again, but there was still a level of mutual respect. He didn't hit me in the face, which is what I was fully expecting. Instead, he grabbed me by my sides, both hands under my armpits. He threw me like a child up and over the reclining chair. I landed on my back with the chair half on my legs. Then he threw the chair aside and started in for round two. He started to swing at my legs and I could tell he wanted to fight me like a man and give me a real ass-whooping, but he was holding back, and I wasn't complaining.

From that night on, things changed for me, and for the first time I feared someone other than the law. That interaction between my dad and me may have been the single most important event in my life in terms of shaping my behavior. My dad did not know at the time that he had helped me for the better. It would come back to bite him in the ass later, but he helped me.

I knew things were different in this new life. People were different. No longer was I in the desert where we had our own code of conduct and the only requirement was to stay out of the back of a cop car. These people were professionals and business owners; they had expectations of their kids and the people around them. It was strange for me to see my father as a successful business owner, because I knew the anger in his heart, and we were more alike than he would ever care to admit. The thing is, my father would fit perfectly into that desert mentality. I think he knew that and it scared him, and I feel that is the main reason he left when I was just one. He was living that life with my mother and he could see how that life traps people. He saw the dependencies getting built in that type of family structure. He knew before long he wouldn't be able to leave it, so he just ripped the Band-Aid off and left.

My dad and I had a similar upbringing. His dad was an alcoholic and beat his mother pretty severely. They grew up poor, and his mom continued to struggle throughout her life financially. He spent his entire life running from his past and is still running to this day. He drives nice cars, self-educates at an extremely high level, and constantly pursues new business ventures. When he owned his bar and restaurant, he fell in love with brewing and won multiple awards for his beers. He was at the leading edge of microbrewing, but unfortunately, those achievements were never enough for him, and I understand now that no achievement will ever be enough. Not until he faces his past and owns it. Only then can the future be rewarding, only when you stop trying to create someone new and learn to love who you are. Only then will you love the path you are on and be excited about your journey.

I had a friend named Bobby over when I was living with my dad, and I'll never forget the next morning when we were leaving my house. Bobby said, "You and your parents are like roommates." I thought that was a strange thing to say, so I asked why he thought that. He said it was strange how we seemed to have no connection; they just do their thing and I do mine. They sit in their office and work; I walk in and occasionally check in like they are a front desk service. Until he made that comment, I hadn't realized how abnormal that was. As I started to think about it, I realized he was right; we were just roommates. The strange thing was, I liked it that way. As long as I wasn't doing anything overtly wrong, they left me alone. I would stop in, and my dad would roll me a cigarette, we'd all have a smoke and chat, then I would be on my way. If only things could have stayed that way.

NO MORE BACKUP

———

Being new in high school was one of the hardest things I ever experienced. My entire life I went to school knowing who people were and having grown up with a lot of them. I didn't realize until the first day at this new school that I was truly on my own. No brother to come fight for me or with me when someone started running their mouth. No backup, no family members, just me.

It didn't take long before I walked through the halls and heard my name called out. I knew instantly that it wasn't good; if you haven't made friends and someone calls you by your name, it only means one thing. I turned around and instantly was punched in the mouth. I took him to the ground and was about to start punching him in the face when I thought about my dad. All I could think about was the real ass-whooping that would follow. So I pinned this guy's hands to the ground, and I could hear kids yelling for a teacher and that there was a fight going on.

I jumped up, left him on the ground, and walked normally down the hall. A teacher asked me if there was a fight, and I said I didn't know, maybe it was that way as I pointed down the hall and kept walking. My adrenaline pumped and I felt like I was going to vomit. I called my dad and had him come pick me up. As I got in the car, he acted like he was a father for the first time in my life. He asked what happened, and I told him about the fight. I assured him I didn't fight back. He asked why not. I thought, is he freaking kidding me, I just let that dude punch me in the face. He said I couldn't go home and that I needed to get back in there and walk around with my head held high and show everyone that he didn't affect me at all.

My mouth had started to swell, but I knew he was right. I went back inside and went to class. I even raised my hand and answered questions to show that I was fine. I wasn't, of course. Just as I raised my hand, I heard a girl behind me whisper that her boyfriend told her he beat my ass. Then she said, "But he looks fine to me." My father's advice was spot-on. I didn't find out until a couple of years later that the same girl told her boyfriend I grabbed her ass because she wanted to see if he would fight for her. How stupid.

Even though my dad's advice was good that day, I'd neglect to listen to him throughout my life. An army chaplain even repeated the same wisdom to me years later after a verbal altercation in Afghanistan. "Never let 'em see you sweat," he told me, but for some reason, I had always struggled with this simple advice. It wasn't until later in life that I started to learn the benefits of keeping your biggest moves a secret, keeping your emotions under control, and allowing others to have the "win" in a disagreement. These power moves are how people utilize their emotions to win in life.

This is a level of discipline that has taken me my entire life to begin to understand. Pay attention to anyone who struggles in life and it will not take long to see that they reveal their emotions clearly and accurately. They are incapable of deception when it comes to how they feel at every moment. Emotions themselves are powerful; however, your ability to control them is key. If everyone knows how you feel at all times, life becomes extremely difficult to control. You become a victim to your emotional responses, and this is how I spent nearly my entire life.

FINDING
MY PLACE

—

It took a while for things to finally start smoothing out at this school. At first, all the rich kids tried to befriend me because my dad owned a restaurant in town. All of these kids' parents owned real estate or had political positions in the community, so I guess they felt like they should clique up. I don't really know. They were good kids, just not my style.

I did find my group and started to do better in school. I wasn't getting in trouble and I was actually passing my classes. Soon after that, I decided I wanted to start a clothing company called Wicked Obsessions. My dad was already buying screen-printing equipment for his own side venture and I convinced him I could sell shirts if he gave me a shot with some start-up money. He helped me out and funded my first order, and it wasn't even two days before all the shirts were sold.

I started contacting stores in the mall and local tattoo shops to get them to start carrying my shirts. It got to the point where people were driving around town with Wicked Obsession stickers on their cars. It felt good and I was proud of what I was building.

I'll never forget the time I approached a guy with a Wicked Obsessions decal on his car and he told me how it was this cool clothing label that a high school kid was running. He didn't believe me when I told him I was that kid. I also ended up meeting a couple of band groupies at a Blink 182 concert who told me about a band named Colors in the Air. I listened to their stuff and loved it, so I contacted them and sponsored the band.

Life seemed like it was really taking off for me, and then my dad dropped a bombshell. He told me we were all moving to Colorado. My dad's wife was traveling to Colorado a lot for work, and they figured it would save them money to move. At first, I thought it was a cool idea because I was never afraid of new challenges and it might be fun. But after some more thought, I remembered how hard it was to start fresh at a new high school. The idea of doing that again made me sick to my stomach. I decided I wasn't going to go, and I honestly thought my dad would support my decision considering how far I had come. I was wrong.

The next time I came home after I told my dad I wasn't moving with him, all my stuff was missing. My clothes, my shoes...they were all gone. My dad told me he gave all my stuff away. That was horrible for me. I was finally starting to fit in at a new school and now I had no clothes. My dad was a very calculated man and was trying to interfere with my social life so I wouldn't want to stay anymore. The clothes incident didn't hurt nearly as much as what came next.

As I walked into my room, the screens that had all of my shirt designs were sitting on the floor. They had been slashed with a knife. He essentially ended my business right then and there, and that hurt. I was so proud of that clothing label and how far it had come and the support I received. For the first time, I felt like I was valuable and my ideas mattered. Then, just like that, I was back to where I started.

Once my dad realized his plan didn't work and I was still sticking with my plan to stay, the cops were knocking at our door. My dad brought me to them and they pulled me aside. They said, "Your dad tells us you're hanging around with a bad crowd." I couldn't believe it. They were actually some of the best people I had met in my life. I asked what they were talking about, and they said my dad told them I was hanging out with Jose something; I recognized the name. He was a gang banger in my school and I hated that guy! He was a lowlife, and what my dad didn't realize is that he actually punched one of my friends in the face for no reason. I could not think of anyone I disliked more than that Jose.

I saw what my dad was doing. I told the cops I didn't hang out with that guy and asked if they had anything else. Once they left, I felt betrayed. I was so hurt by this. All of the shit my mother put me through was easier to deal with because at the end of the day, she was an addict. She had a problem and was led by her addiction. My father was an intelligent, successful man, yet he was pulling the same crap my mother did. I could not believe I had to deal with the same kind of games. The same manipulation that my dad claimed to hate so much about my mother, and he was using it on me.

I moved in with a friend, and the cops showed up telling me I had to go back. I'd had enough. I asked my dad flat out what he thought was going to happen and how he thought he was going to keep me with him. I knew that he could not possibly think he could control me after everything he watched me go through. He finally said that he would only let me leave if I found family to stay with, not friends. His mother was the only person I knew in the area. He hadn't talked to her in years, so it was a long shot, but I went straight to her house and the joke was on him. She was an awesome lady and let me move in with her. She lived far from my school, so I waited for my dad to move out before I went back to live with friends.

One day after moving back to Fredonia to be with my friends, I decided to take a walk past my dad's old house. It was raining really hard and I walked by the empty house with a "For Sale" sign in the front yard. I sat on the back porch in the rain, and for the first time in years I felt sorry for myself. I felt abandoned. I couldn't understand why my dad and his wife felt the need to lash out at me. Why couldn't they understand that I had to live my own life? They celebrated my ability to stick with my plans, and they celebrated my move from California; yet now they were cursing me, and all I was doing was sticking with my plans again.

I sat there in the rain feeling like shit. I felt alone and started to question whether I had made the right decision. It seemed like the weather was supporting me at that moment, like the rain was a representation of my struggle and I needed that. I needed a moment to just feel like shit. After moving from California and leaving my entire family, hating my new school and struggling to fit in, and now my dad trying to sabotage my progress for his own. I allowed it all to hit me—I allowed the pity to stay in my heart for a few minutes. Finally, it stopped. The problem solver in me had enough, and he went to work.

I got up from the back porch and thought, "Fuck this, I'm going to stay on my path." I realized the best thing I could do was prove to both my parents I was better off without them. I didn't need them to survive, and I damn sure wasn't going to end up failing on my own. I knew when my dad left he would be waiting to hear my name come up as being arrested or dropping out of school. In that small town, he was well known; it would only be a matter of time before any mistake would be reported back to him. I wasn't going to give him the satisfaction. He was fucking wrong, and I was going to prove it.

That moment was powerful for me, allowing me to

stop fighting for a second and accept the way I felt. We are all human and struggle with our feelings, especially during times of hardship. It is important to push through and keep moving forward, but at some point, it can be a powerful release to just give yourself the freedom to feel it all. Open the floodgates and feel the pain and sadness. Allow the overwhelming amount of pity to take over for a brief moment. Feel it, feel all of it, then take a deep breath, and get back in the game.

I never talked about what was going on in my life with anyone. Nobody knew what I was going through or had been through. This moment of sadness was my cup overflowing and me reaching a breaking point. Yet, instead of losing control, I simply just allowed the cup to overflow and felt completely rejuvenated afterward. We forget as adults the importance of this emotional release, and we continue to fight through it until the release is no longer within our control. Then the release manifests itself as road rage or a fight with your spouse. It makes us feel powerless, and we are destined to repeat it.

After that, I stayed on anyone's couch if they let me. I knew the game: parents let you stay until they were sick of you, then asked you to go home. I didn't care.

While I was couch hopping, I was also studying and getting my grades up. One of my good friends had a mom who treated me like her own. She had one rule: go to school, and you can stay here until you graduate; stop going to school, and you're out. I was so grateful for her and the way she treated me. For Christmas our senior year, she got my friend and me matching class rings. She made me realize that blood relationships were irrelevant in life—people either choose to be in your life or they don't.

I not only got my act together and graduated high school; I passed some extra tests and was awarded a regent's diploma. Graduation day came, and my girlfriend at the time brought her parents to make it look like I had family at graduation. Their support was awesome and they were great people, but I honestly wish I had been alone. I wish I had just gone by myself as a symbol to my parents that I had what it took to make things happen on my own. It was a victory for me and it felt good.

When I left California, I was failing school and fully expected to be a high school dropout, but my dad put some fear into me. I took the discipline that came from that fear and made it my own. I stood there throwing that cap in the air knowing that from that point on, my life was my own.

FROM PAIN
COMES POWER

—

I ENDED UP MARRYING THE GIRL WHO CAME TO MY GRAD-
uation. That brings us back to me walking in on her
with another man. The few days that followed shook
me to my core—they awoke my senses and kicked me
right in the balls. There are certain things in life that
we are just not prepared to deal with, and unfortunately, those things are going to happen. When they
do, they shatter you to the core and bring you to a new
low. This was one of those moments for me, but now
I understand why I was able to pick myself up and get
back on track. I had years of practice picking myself
back up. My childhood had prepared me to get kicked
in the nuts and move on.

We all have traumas in our lives that prepare us to be strong. We learn more than we know about life and obstacles through those experiences. The problem is, we never learn how to use them. Nobody ever teaches us how to embrace the past and use it to our advantage. People are so attached to the words of Friedrich Nietzsche—"That which does not kill us, makes us stronger"—yet we assume that the strength will just develop after hard times. We figure the tough times happened and therefore the strength is already working to our advantage. Unfortunately, that is not the case. Because we bury it deep down and do everything we can to ignore it, we fail to accept the gift. We must face our traumas and acknowledge the impact it has had on us. Once we face our trauma, it becomes a tool to be utilized. My tool manifested in the form of a dragon, and the more trauma I endured, the larger my dragon grew. I could feel its power, I could feel its hunger, but I was ashamed of it.

I spent years running from it. That dragon represented my poverty, pain, and a strong feeling of inadequacy. I spent a large part of my life feeling stupid and extremely undereducated. My dragon embarrassed me, so I ran from it. Every time I would think I got away, my anger acted up, or I would become embarrassed of my shortcomings and lash out. When you are vulnerable, angry, or upset, your dragon takes over and all of your unresolved "issues" are front and center for everyone to see. I would convince myself that I outran my dragon and therefore he was no longer part of me, but then my emotions would get the best of me. I would try to fight, curse someone out, or just act plain broken and my ruse would come falling apart. This is where the medals and achievements came in.

I tried to use medals and achievements to prove to everyone else that I was someone I wasn't. The marathons, the degrees, the awards—they were all proof that I escaped my dragon and became "better." None of those things made me better. I had to learn to tame my dragon and use it. Once I did that, I realized I was not only the man I wanted to be; I was far more. I had it within me the entire time; the real success was just waiting to be unleashed.

We all have a dragon within us, and the more trauma you have faced in your life, the larger and more powerful that dragon is. If you have never learned to tame your dragon or even acknowledge its existence, then you are failing to utilize life's most powerful tool. If you have been stuck in a loop of behavior that you struggle to change, or if you seem to ruin opportunities and feel saddened by the way your life has developed, it is a sign that you need to go back and figure out what made your dragon powerful. It is time to dig out the memories that you have subconsciously suppressed and chosen to forget. It's time to face your past and find out why your trauma is the best thing that's ever happened to you.

GROWING PAIN

—

AFTER I RECOVERED FROM MY EX CHEATING ON ME, I knew I had to grow. I knew I had to be better in order to win over this trauma. The problem was, I still had not faced my past. So I would make progress, then knock myself back down. The last straw came when I decided I wanted to be a firefighter. I signed up for college and started taking all of the prerequisite courses to attend the fire academy. California is different in that a large amount of the training is considered to be prerequisites. You have to complete multiple college courses before putting in an application for the fire academy. I had finished all of the classes, wildland fire academy, confined space awareness, and the others. The last step was EMT basic, and I signed up for an accelerated course to get it done as soon as possible.

The road was tough, but I was doing well. I got rides from a guy I met at the course because my car was starting to break down. The guy was a skater and very small, maybe 125 pounds. One day, he came up to me during the break and says that one of the other students, an ex-army guy, wanted to fight him. I asked why would he want that. He said he had no idea; the guy just kept looking at him angrily and making comments about kicking his ass when he walks by. I told my friend he was probably misreading the situation and not to worry about it. We went back to class. I got up to throw away my gum in the trash, and as I looked down at the guy, sure enough he was giving me the stink eye now. I stopped and said, "What the fuck is your problem?" He said, "I'll see you at break." I thought, fine with me.

We had uniforms and I was supposed to be wearing boots, but I decided that Crocs would be more comfortable that day. I asked my friend to switch me shoes so I didn't have to fight in Crocs. We switched, and break came shortly after. I walked outside and got ready to fight this guy; he walked up to me and put his nose in my forehead. His nose actually touched my forehead. First, I thought that was gross, and then I headbutted him in the nose as hard as I could. Fight was over; his nose started gushing blood. Apparently, he had a girlfriend in class because she started screaming like he was going to bleed to death.

The teacher came out and called us upstairs. We both told the same story—nothing happened and his nose was an accident. She said we were not allowed to return to school until a "formal investigation" was completed. I asked how long that would take, because you could miss only two days of this course. She said longer than two days. I thought well, that is it. I can't keep doing this to myself. Every time I start to get ahead, I sabotage my progress. I was my own worst enemy, and I was tired of screwing it up. It was time for some drastic measures; I needed help getting my shit together.

This moment was just one of many where my untamed dragon took control of my life. I had never taken the time to see that it even existed, let alone learn how and why it was there. Yet, there he was, destroying everything I was achieving again. It was the same pattern on a continual loop of self-sabotage. I had to change it, but I did not yet know how. So I did the one thing I did know: find some more traumas to overcome.

The next morning, I walked into the military recruiter's

office. First, the air force wouldn't give me a chance for having too many tattoos, then the marines, same response. Then the army, the guy asked what I wanted to do. I told him the Rangers sounded high speed and I wanted to be a Ranger. He said too easy; come back tomorrow and we'll see what we can do. I spent about five minutes in that office, which should have been a clue that I needed to spend more time thinking about this decision and what job I really wanted. But I wasn't going to let myself overthink this decision. I knew I wanted to go and that was what I was going to do.

The next morning, I went back to the recruiter with my hopes high that he was able to land me a Ranger contract. He sat me down and said he had some good news and some bad news. He said we got your Ranger and Airborne School contract; however, unfortunately, they are not accepting Ranger contracts for infantry at this time, so you will have to go on initially as a 92G Food Service Specialist. All I heard was that my contract said "Ranger" and "Airborne." I asked how long I would have to be a cook before being able to switch to infantry. He told me to get into Ranger battalion, and they would let me switch to infantry within six months. I knew I could do any job for six months and be okay; I told him I was ready to go.

In basic training, I learned quickly that the army was not going to change who I was. I was hoping the army would be a place for me to be myself, rough around the edges, and I would be accepted. However, I learned quickly that even by army standards, I was out of control.

During one incident, I was walking through a rival company's sleeping bay to get to our classroom. The company had their combative mats laid out all over the floor and were watching for people to step on them so they could talk some shit. I bumped into a buddy and stepped on it for a quick second before getting right back off. One of the guys immediately started cussing me out, telling me to stay off their fucking mats. So instead of walking past and going to class, my dragon took over yet again.

I stopped and looked him in the eye. Then, with about five guys standing in a group waiting for a fight, I stood on their mat and spit on it. All of them ran toward me, and I was able to take one to the ground shortly before my drill sergeant screamed my name and everyone stopped. I thought, "Well, this didn't last long. I guess it's time to go back to California." My drill sergeant asked me what happened. I told him exactly what I did. He looked at me slightly confused, then yelled at the guys I was fighting to fuck off. He looked me in the eyes and then just calmly told me to cut the shit and to stay off people's mats. I knew instantly that any other drill sergeant would have taken me down for review. But this guy saw something in me and let the whole thing go. Despite what people may think, fighting in basic is not okay. I should have at least been punished.

After that came AIT (Advanced Individual Training) where I learned to cook eggs and iron cook whites. I'll never forget showing up to AIT and seeing people march around in cook whites. I asked the guy next to me, "What the fuck are they wearing?" He said proudly, "That's our uniform! We wear those instead of the Army Combat Uniform." Ah, fuck me! I didn't want to be caught dead in that shit, and I knew right then and there I made a huge mistake. I decided I would do anything to get out of this job and get into something I actually wanted to do.

Then, finally after about four months, the stuff I signed up for came around. Airborne School was a terrifying blast; they have a cadence they sing about your first jump. It talks about your knees getting weak and knocking together. They weren't joking either. During my first jump standing there with the door open knowing I had to jump out, my legs started quivering and turning to Jell-O. Part of me hoped they would cancel the jump and we would land and walk off that bird. Instead, the jumpmaster stared at us with a little evil grin and yelled, "GO! GOO! GOOOO!" and the guy in front of me disappeared. My wobbly legs kept taking steps forward despite me wanting to turn around and run to the back of the plane. Then it was my turn. I closed my eyes, chin down, hands on my reserve shoot, and stepped out.

Training is a valuable tool—when you want to quit or are too afraid to think, it kicks in and gives you something to focus on. Jumping out of a plane for the first time hoping not to die is terrifying. But you are trained to focus on keeping your chin down, hands on your reserve, jump, keep your feet together, count to five, and check for a good opening. All of those things are simple tasks and are not scary. What Airborne School was teaching me was to follow directions over fear. When shit gets really scary and you are truly afraid of failure or death, just follow instructions. It is hard to think about your parachute failing to open and plunging to your death when you are following basic instructions step by step.

This can be true for every goal in your life: make a plan and stick to it. When things get scary and failure is likely, focus on the steps you have to take, and do them one at a time. That focus takes up too much room for your imagination to dwell on the possibilities of failure.

I finished Airborne School landing like a sack of potatoes most of the time but without injuries. They pinned our "blood wings" (airborne wings) to our chest by punching them into our skin after graduation. Proud family members were allowed to pin the wings to their sons, brothers, and family. I waited as dad after dad stepped up to pin on their sons' wings. The cadre got to me and asked if I had anyone to pin my wings, and I said, "No," with confidence and pride.

He gently placed my wings on my chest before punching them hard. I could feel the prongs of the wings pierce my skin and the blood soak into my shirt. I smiled inside and welled with pride to have taken part in the tradition. The army is all about tradition because it connects those who serve now with those who served in the past. It's a reminder that we are all there for a larger, more important purpose than ourselves. I didn't know it at the time, but that connection would be exactly what I needed.

We were all riding a graduation high. For some of us, that high was about to come crashing down in a major way. The Airborne cadre had us all in one large formation. He said, "Congratulations to all of you. Some of you will now start vacation before heading to your new units. If that is you, make a separate formation over here." The majority of our formation split off and was now standing next to us. The cadres then looked at the rest of us and said, "For some reason, you idiots signed up to be Rangers. Your day will now get a whole lot worse. The Ranger cadre is running down here now to pick you up. Grab all of your shit and wait for them to arrive. Good luck."

Next thing I knew, there was a six four, jacked dude in all black workout clothes running toward us. We immediately knew that we were screwed. This guy was square-jawed and had a lip full of dip—he was not playing. He instantly started yelling for us to grab our shit and follow him. Grab my shit? I have a backpack and two full army duffel bags. Where's the truck? I grabbed all the shit I had and, barely hanging on, tried to follow this psychopath. We finally made it to the top of a hill and saw the infamous brown fence. We formed up behind one of the cadre huts and shit hit the fan. At one point, we were holding our bags over our heads for so long the guy in front of me puked all over himself.

GUT CHECK

Rangers and Green Berets have a very different approach to tearing a man down. Although both are extremely effective, they have different expected outcomes, and the torture is tailored to those outcomes. The Rangers canceled my August start date because the heat and humidity in Georgia were too much. They would have to temper their abuse to avoid the entire group falling out as heat casualties. This was bad news for us because it meant living in the Ranger huts and getting our balls smoked off daily as we waited for the next class to start. Then another kick in the nuts came when we found out that author and Navy SEAL Dick Couch was writing a book on our class and he would be shadowing the entire thing. I don't care who you are, but if someone shows up to write a book on how tough your training is, it's going to get even tougher.

Training day finally came and things were off to a good start. I passed the swim test and started to find a rhythm early on. I performed at my max effort whenever I was waiting for someone to finish an iteration. If there was even a second of downtime, I pulled out my Ranger handbook and shoved my face in it. But the next day, things went south for me. We got all geared up for a ruck run and the goal was to stay within an arm's length of the guy in front of you at all times. I was doing just that; this guy was not going to leave my arm's length no matter what!

Then, suddenly, out of nowhere, the cadre was running next to me. I could feel his eyes burning into the side of my head. Full of anger and aggression, he yelled at me to look in front of the man I was following. I looked in front of him and noticed that he had fallen way behind. The cadre yelled for me to close the gap. I took off running down the Fort Benning hill as fast as I possibly could. My rucksack started to swing back and forth, and before I knew it, my right ankle twisted and popped. I slid along the asphalt, scraping holes on my knees and elbows. I didn't realize it at the time, but I was groaning in pain.

The next thing I know, the cadre is standing over me

telling me to shut the fuck up and keep moving. So I bit my lip to stop the moans of pain, got up, and limped my way back to the front of the pack. Dick Couch ran up and tried to interview me about my fall, but I was in too much pain to respond. He moved on, and that was the last I would see of him.

That run was powerful for me because I knew I was injured, but I would not stop running. I could feel the tendons swell and spike with pain with every step. The truck full of kids who had quit the march passed me, and I just wanted to keep going. I convinced myself that if I could just finish the ruck march, my ankle would be fine.

We got back to the barracks and were told to change out and bring everything we owned outside. I went to take off my right boot and it wouldn't come off. I had to untie my laces and completely remove them before my boot would even slide off. I took off my sock and saw my ankle was already turning black, all the way to my toes. The swelling was incredible. It was so bad my foot had no shape; it was just a fat stump. I limped downstairs, and the cadre looked at my ankle and calmly said, "Well...you're done."

This was a huge loss for me. The only thing I wanted

was to be a Ranger. I wanted that scroll so badly. I dreamed about wearing that tan beret, and the opportunity had passed me by. The master sergeant called me into his office and told me I was the type of guy they were looking for and wanted me to come back when I healed up. Those words meant the world to me—someone I had immense respect for telling me I was the type of guy they wanted, when I didn't even know what type of guy I was. I was there to try and figure that out and see what I really had to give.

It was a strange time in my life as a young man. I signed up for something not knowing whether I had what it took to succeed. I still didn't know where my place was in the world, and I had spent so much time failing due to my own stupid mistakes. At this time, I was still running from my past, and I had not accepted the victories of my youth. I had not acknowledged the strength and determination I had acquired from my past. All I wanted was to know what my current strengths were, and I needed to know that I could be valuable.

I left the Rangers on crutches. I developed Achilles tendinitis in my right ankle from the injury and it was extremely prone to rolling, which caused an immense amount of pain. After the Rangers, I went to 173rd

Airborne in Bamberg Germany, and it seemed I was back to being my old self. I was just drinking and fighting, waiting to sabotage this new career with stupid childish mistakes. It was then that I met my second wife, and she became pregnant with our daughter shortly after. The birth of my daughter changed me, and I knew I had to get back on track and get my shit together. I was a cook and hated it with a passion, and I had to change my circumstances or I was going to deploy in a job I hated. If that happened, I wouldn't get anything I expected from this experience.

I heard the command sergeant major's (CSM's) personal security was moving to another base, and I knew this could be the opportunity I was looking for. I knew that this position was not given to cooks and I would have to be a little unorthodox in my approach. The thing about unorthodox and the military is that there really is no such thing. Being unorthodox pisses people off because the chain of command wants you to do everything through them without question. Fortunately for me, I was perfectly fine with pissing people off.

I waited for the CSM to go through the breakfast line, and I made sure I was serving so I could talk to him personally. I was lined up ready to strike, but then I saw my first sergeant standing right next to him. I thought, "Shit, I was hoping to go behind his back and not do this right in front of him!" Oh well, I wanted that job, and he was not going to intimidate me out of trying.

When the CSM made it to my line, I came right out with it. "Sergeant Major, I heard you needed a soldier for your personal security detachment [PSD]." He said, "I do, but we tend not to pull those from cooks." Just then, I could feel the heat and anger coming from my first sergeant. I just avoided eye contact with him and went on with my speech. I said, "Sir, with the deployment to Afghanistan coming up, you need a PSD that can perform. I will physically outperform and outshoot any other candidate going for that spot."

He looked at me, looked at my first sergeant, and made the decision right then and there. "He's got a point, First Sergeant. He's my new PSD." I was elated, but of course my first sergeant wasn't about to let that happen. So no movement came, and the sergeant in charge of me started treating me like shit. I knew I was catching the tail end of the stunt I pulled, and my first sergeant was going to make my life a living hell for it.

Shortly after the incident, we had a field rotation out

in the woods. While all the cooks were prepping kitchens and cooking food, I was in a dirt ditch known as a foxhole that I spent an entire two weeks improving at the order of my first sergeant. I did nothing but dig that hole the entire trip. After coming back to the base, I was once again serving breakfast, and I could see the command sergeant major walking in with my first sergeant. This time, my first sergeant had a smug look on his face—he thought his little digging escapade would have whipped me into shape. But he clearly did not know me.

As soon as the CSM got to me, the first sergeant stood by his side, glaring at me with contempt. I said, "Sergeant Major, didn't you want me to be your PSD?" He looked at me, a little confused before saying, "That's right. Hey, First Sergeant, make sure he transfers over right now." First Sergeant said, "Roger, Sergeant Major." I wanted to take off the cook whites and throw them in the first sergeant's face. I could not believe it; I just got myself out of the job I hated and into something far better. It was a huge risk that nearly cost me a lot of pain, but it worked.

This meant that during the upcoming deployment, I wouldn't be stuck in a kitchen. Instead, I would be with the CSM and traveling around the country to visit his guys. That was a calculated risk because if I failed, I would ruin my chances of promotion by pissing off nearly my entire chain of command. This mattered and was worth the risk. To this day, it was one of the best jobs I have ever had.

My CSM looked out for his people; he was a great leader and a great mentor. He taught me a lot about leading by example and making tough decisions for the benefit of those underneath you. I would watch him struggle with making the right decision for his people, then he never took credit for the countless hours he spent worrying about their well-being. He didn't do the job for the recognition. He would never tell the people that he was the one making the call to send them home for funerals or the births of their children. He never told them he put them in for award after award, or how he would send their noncommissioned officer evaluation reports back because they didn't properly portray the value of the soldier. These reports determined a noncommissioned officer's career path, and a great one can ensure the job you want. A bad one can ruin a soldier's chances for military advancement. The list goes on and on. This guy was a true leader, and everything he taught me stayed with me throughout my career.

During that deployment, I wanted to test myself as much as I could. When we weren't on mission traveling to bases so the CSM could check on his soldiers, I would go to the med station and wait for injured soldiers to be flown in. This was where the action was on the base, and that's where I wanted to be. I was fortunate the CSM supported me in this, so whenever I heard the radio call out with injured incoming, I would race over to help out. At that point, I was healed from my injury and getting back into shape. I decided that instead of going back to Ranger selection, I would try Special Forces Assessment and Selection. I trained hard while I was out there with two-a-day CrossFit workouts followed by lots of miles with the ruck on.

Then, one day, the radio announced two injured soldiers coming in to the medical station. I jumped into the CSM's truck and raced down there. When I arrived, there were two Green Berets being pulled off the bird. I ran back with the medical staff who were working on them. One guy had through-and-through bullet wounds through the back of both of his legs. He was sitting next to his teammate who was no longer being worked on. His teammate was killed in action and his lifeless body lay there waiting to be removed by the mortuary affairs sergeant.

The Green Beret looked at me right in the eyes with a glazed look about him. It was as though he didn't realize his friend was lying there dead or that his own legs were full of holes. He just sat there calm and emotionless, looking at me, and I had nothing to offer him. I had done nothing in my life that could compare to what he had just gone through. This man was a true hero. I was so taken aback by the courage of these guys that I had not yet realized how they changed me.

The mortuary affairs sergeant and the chaplain came in just then to move the body and start processing him for his hero ceremony. I helped move the body, and we wheeled him back to the Mortuary Affairs office. We folded an American flag and stapled it to his body bag. The flag had two gold medal rings attached to it. The chaplain cut them off; just then, he looked at the rings in his hands and looked at me. He handed me one of the rings and said, "Are you sure you want to do this?" I had never been surer about anything in my entire life. I had no idea if I was a good man or capable of being a Green Beret, but I knew I needed to try. I kept that ring in my front right pocket, close to my heart, as a symbol that good men will perish and they rely on other good men to take their place. That ring was removed from the flag of fallen hero Green Beret SFC Riley G. Stephens. SFC Stephens died September 28, 2012, from small-arms fire in Wardak Province, Afghanistan.

Looking back, I realize that at this point in my life, my dragon had grown to be a massive devastating force. I still had not figured out how to train it—it was just a force that was there, hungry and mean. I could feel how powerful it was but had no confidence in how to direct its power. Sometimes, it was there to help me win; other times, it was there to burn down every bridge I needed to cross. I could never tell when it would work in my favor, or when it would ruin everything I had accomplished. I was afraid of it, and I was afraid that my past was the part of me that was causing the destruction. In my mind, I separated my choices and behavior into two separate categories: the stuff I did wrong was a result of my childhood, and my successes were the result of the growth I had made.

SPECIAL FORCES ASSESSMENT AND SELECTION

—

I WAS GEARING UP TO FACE THE BIGGEST CHALLENGE OF my life, and I was terrified. Special Forces Assessment and Selection (SFAS) was where men went to see what they were made of. It was known to take some of the toughest men and break them down mentally and physically. It was instant respect for anyone who made it to the end. I had not just watched the show *Surviving the Cut*, which documented an SFAS class; I also studied it. I watched the people struggle. I watched people try and take shortcuts. I studied the map they posted in the show, hoping it would give me an advantage. The show scared the shit out of me. I watched these guys giving everything they had, and a lot of them still didn't make it. I just wanted to know if I had what it took, and I wanted to know if a braver man would look at me and see potential. I could only imagine that by twenty-two years old, confidence should have come from a father or from family, but I was seeking it on my own. I was desperate for someone I respected to tell me I was good enough.

Heading to SFAS, I tried to block the fear out of my mind. I tried to ignore the fact that the hardest three weeks of my life were about to happen. SFAS is probably the first time I had really noticed the mindset differences of people who succeed in that type of environment. Some of us put every ounce of energy into thinking about the task at hand, whereas others lived in the future. Those who lived in the future welled up with fear and allowed those fears to dictate their behavior, whereas those who just focused on that very moment had no time to worry about the future. We put our heads down and tried our absolute best right then and there.

The interesting thing was, most people weren't hitting their breaking points under the insane amounts of weight and miles we were enduring. They hit their breaking points when we got back to the barracks and they had time to think. That was when things got really hard for people; you could see the panic set in about what the next day would bring, and I was no different in that regard. Every single night, I thought to myself, "How can I do another day of this? How can I possibly have the strength to keep up at this pace?" However, instead of letting the fear creep into my mind, I thought about a friend who had been selected. He did it, he woke up the next day, sucked it up, and completed the next day; and if he could do it, then maybe I could, too.

One day after we got back from a weeklong team event, a buddy was looking outside the barracks just staring into space. I asked him if everything was okay, and he said if it was raining outside tomorrow, he was done. I laughed it off and went to bed. I thought he was just trying to get himself through the fear of tomorrow by giving himself a mental out. I thought for sure he would forget about it in the morning and move on. But the next morning, I woke up and his bunk was cleared. He had gotten up in the middle of the night and packed his stuff. I looked outside and it was raining.

Each person who quit gave me a sense of encouragement. It made me feel for a quick second that maybe, just maybe, that burning in my soul is something real, maybe it is something that is actually powerful. Day in and day out, people were dropping like flies, but I was still there and that meant the world to me.

One infamous event in selection is called the down pilot. It is an apparatus that has to be built by the candidates. The apparatus represents a downed-pilot rescue. The only difference is, this apparatus weighs what feels like a ton. I could not even guess how much that stupid thing adds up to, and we fit as many guys underneath it as possible to share the load. The weight was causing so much pain in my hips that I could feel the joint wanting to come out of the socket with each step. This thing was not breaking my mind, but I could feel it trying to tear my body apart. Then, just as we thought it couldn't get any harder, I looked up and saw the sand hill. It was a steep climb covered in beach sand and, from the bottom, looked impossible to climb with all of the weight. It must have been the length of two football fields covered in a foot of sand. The climb would have been challenging with just our rucksacks alone, and now we had this big thing on top of it all.

This is when your mind takes one of two paths: stare at

the hill and determine it cannot be done, or look down at your feet, pretend it's not there, and take one step at a time. The latter is what I chose to do; I kept taking steps until they told me I was done. The last event was with a rucksack filled with water weighing sixty to sixty-five pounds and a ruck march for an undisclosed distance. From what we learned about the area, we figured the distance was between twenty-two to twenty-five miles. I thought finishing that ruck would bring a huge sense of pride and accomplishment. Unfortunately, all I could think about was whether I did all of it for nothing.

We waited outside the cadre hut in a formation. This was when they were going to sit you down and tell you what they observed over the last three weeks and then finish with whether you were selected. It was time for a Green Beret to look me in the eyes and tell me whether he felt I was worthy. That kind of judgment was terrifying for me, and as someone who was unsure of who I was or what my purpose was, that moment was everything. I waited, pacing back and forth for what felt like hours. They finally called my roster number. I had a huge knot in my throat and could barely breathe. As I walked toward the Green Beret, he had a paper in his hand, and I was sure it was a list of my shortcomings.

As soon as I approached him, he said, "You want the long or the short version?" I asked for the short version, and he said I had been selected and to get the fuck out of there. I couldn't control the loud burst of excitement that came rushing out of me. The instructor smirked and yelled, "I SAID, GET THE FUCK OUT OF HERE!" I just ran away. I sat down on a bench and became overwhelmed with pride. It was one of the most powerful moments in my life. For the first time ever, I had accomplished something that made me feel powerful and different. I had just proven to myself that I might have what it takes; the fire burning inside me just might be real.

ONE STEP CLOSER

I WENT HOME WITH A VICTORY UNDER MY BELT. THE plane ride back to Germany felt incredible. I felt like a new man, but I also felt cautious. I knew that with ups came downs, and I would have a long way to go before anyone would award me a Green Beret. But on that plane ride, I did something different—I let myself have the victory. I did not let the fear creep in that I would inevitably screw this up. I just enjoyed thinking that maybe I did have what it takes.

I went home, packed up the family, and we all moved to North Carolina for the Special Forces Qualification Course. This course is long and tough, and the hardest part of this course is consistency. Getting it right once in a while was not enough. You had to be on time, at your best, and ready to perform at ALL times. The Q course was teaching us that you had to put up at all times no matter what. Nobody cares about your excuses; you are either getting the job done and accomplishing the mission, or you're out.

That course was life defining for me. There seemed to be a pattern during each school that made my confidence grow. Despite being scared shitless of failure 24/7, I was actually doing well. I kept finding myself in leadership positions throughout the course.

There was a common theme when it came to taking on leadership roles in a high-stress capacity. At first, it is absolutely terrifying and you feel like you were dealt a hard blow. But then something changes; you start to get the hang of it. Your confidence starts to grow and you see the opportunities for looking out for your people. Then the craziest thing happens: your leadership time comes to an end. Instead of feeling relief, I always felt saddened. I loved leading men, helping them reach their potential, and more than anything, I loved earning their trust.

It became addicting, as there was a certain art or finesse

about leading highly aggressive, highly achieved individuals. They empower you to push your own limits; they seek a challenge and look to their leaders to step up to the plate. They don't need you, not even a little. What they need is a new perspective and a new way to challenge their own abilities.

When you're attempting to lead highly skilled individuals, it is common to feel inadequate or inferior. However, it is vital that you understand those emotions and respond to them correctly. You may feel like you want to jump right into the team and show them what you know. You want to prove to them you are worth your weight. However, this can be a costly mistake. When leading some of the best and brightest, you have to swallow your insecurity and allow them to teach you. Understand that you have just as much if not more to learn from them than they have to learn from you. This approach earns their respect; it shows them that you value them and their experience.

A leader's role is not to be the best and brightest in the room at all times—it is to be a conduit for your team. It is to put yourself on the chopping block so they don't have to. I would have never passed the qualification course if it weren't for the dudes around me. Robin sage is the culminating exercise of the Q course. It is an opportunity to put all of your skills to the test and then push your limits. I was given the leadership role of team sergeant during part of that phase and given my own operation to plan and run. We were to conduct a targeted hit on an enemy-guarded communication tower. We moved up on a line with seven men to my left and seven men to my right. Our guerilla force were guys who just started the Q course, so they had not yet gotten all of the training. Even the guys with prior experience were instructed to keep that experience to themselves to add pressure to the guys going through the training.

A good friend of mine and I were going to initiate the hit. We had all crept through the night being as stealthy as possible to avoid being detected by the guards. We got on line and prepared to initiate the assault. I had my guys set: I could see a white light in the distance, but it was too dark to see the target itself. My buddy told me that we were a few degrees off where the target location should have been. I thought that could've been an easy mistake to make with our map calculations, but I was still confident we were lined up on the tower. He took another azimuth and said, "Bro, it's your call, but I think that's our target over there; they probably just blacked the sight out."

I had a decision to make that could cost us the mission and possibly our careers. I decided to trust my friend, and we initiated the raid. He was spot-on. The mission went off without a hitch—almost, until we were running back to the exfiltration point and I looked at one of the guerilla's 249 machine guns and realized it had no barrel. My stomach sank and I grabbed his arm. I said, "Where the fuck is your barrel?" He looked at his weapon and just said, "Oh, shit." I could have killed him.

I ran as fast as I could back to the target location, and there it was, sitting right in the middle of the target. I grabbed it and ran as fast as I possibly could. I felt like Benny from *The Sandlot*; I was fucking cruising. I made it back to the exfil location and sat in the back of the bread van that we paid to get us around without being identified. I was full of pride and looked at my guys who were all celebrating because they knew we were one step closer to earning our berets after a solid performance. I owed that entire mission to my friend who prevented me from conducting a raid on the wrong location and going back with our tails between our legs and our future in question.

My friend could have easily kept his mouth shut; he could have let me fail, knowing it was my neck on the line on that mission. He could have used my failure as an opportunity to look better when it was his turn to lead, but he didn't. The course was full of moments like these: guys looking out for each other no matter if they were in charge or not. We learned to look out for each other, and we learned that success was never a solo mission. In order to succeed, you had to rely on the guys around you, and they would rely on you, too.

Graduating the Q course and donning my Green Beret was one of the proudest moments of my life. I remember the chaplain handed me the gold ring off the flag of SFC Riley G. Stephens on graduation day. That day was like an oath for me; I needed to see it through. I needed to pay my respects by stepping into Stephens's world and doing my absolute best while I was there. For the first time in my life, I had achieved something that was unarguably difficult. I had done something that few men ever get the opportunity to do, and it was time to finally accept that I had what it took. However, wearing the Green Beret was not enough. I still had one more mission to accomplish in order to get a glimpse of what SFC Stephens had gone through—I needed to go to war.

I felt like war was the great equalizer of men. War doesn't care if you're tall or short. It does not judge you, and it does not base its outcome on the quality of your youth. War couldn't care less if you grew up in a trailer on welfare. I wanted desperately to walk onto the battlefield and see what was truly inside. I spent my entire life walking around with a chip on my shoulder, always feeling like I had something to prove, getting into fights, never backing down, and trying to achieve more. It was this lingering feeling of inadequacy that haunted me. I could not escape it, no matter what I did or whom I fought, even after earning my Green Beret and seeing the younger guys look up to me. A lot of people look at that beret and think we somehow transcended to a higher level of badass. In reality, we were all just trying to prove desperately to ourselves that we belonged. Inside, I was scared. I was scared that I was a fake, and deep down, I was waiting to be exposed. I thought I needed to see combat; I needed to face the enemy and prove to myself that I had nothing more to prove to anyone. Soon I was going to get my chance.

"BUCK"

—

I FINALLY GOT ASSIGNED TO AN OPERATIONAL DETACH-
ment Alpha (ODA), 0226. I walked down the hall to
introduce myself to my new team. I was excited and
nervous to finally meet the guys I would be training
and deploying with. These guys were going to be like
my family, and I couldn't wait to meet them. I walked
in as though I would be greeted by an accepting family
and started my speech. "Hey, guys, my name is Sean
Rogers. I am your new 18B!" There were about five
Green Berets in the room and not one of them even
glanced in my direction. I stood there awkwardly waiting for one of them to realize I was even in the room.
Finally, the team medic pointed at one of the operators
sitting in a chair and said, "Team sergeant's right there;
talk to him." So I walked up to the team sergeant and
stood at parade rest (parade rest is a military position

of respect used when talking to people of higher rank). The team sergeant continued to ignore me as I stood there for what felt like an hour. Finally, he looked up at me and said, "Don't stand at parade rest for me; it's fucking weird." Then he said, "What's your name?" I thought, this motherfucker, he wasn't playing, he legitimately ignored everything I just said. I repeated, "Sean Rogers, Sergeant" and he said, "Rogers? Like Buck Rogers?" and then chuckled and went back to ignoring me. Unfortunately, for me the nickname Buck stuck ever since that day. My new guy time was like drinking through a fire hose every day. I was doing everything in my power to be the best 18B I could be. For all of my hard work and effort, I was graciously forced to wear a bright neon yellow hat that read, "0226 FNG" (Fucking New Guy). I fucking hated that hat and worked my ass off to convince the team I was no longer deserving of it. Despite not having a lot of combat experience on the team, we were young and eager for combat.

Special Forces units are divided up into different groups; each group has a primary regional responsibility. My company in 10th Special Forces Group was mostly deploying to Africa when I arrived. However, a couple of months after I got there, they were reassigned to Afghanistan as the primary region. This was going to be the first time our battalion was really going to see continuous combat in years, and we could feel the pressure. My team trained relentlessly for the deployment. We would run live shoot houses for twenty-four hours straight until finally the team sergeant had to call it. Our shot group, which is the group of holes created after shooting the target repeatedly, was getting dangerously big in the early hours of the morning. We had pushed our limits with sleep deprivation and shooting—someone was going to get hurt. But we kept up the pace; we would always be the first team out and the last team back.

We were a young team and most of us had no Special Operations combat experience, so we supplemented the lack of combat with tough, relentless training. It paid off, and by the time we were set to deploy, our team was well oiled and ready.

As an 18B weapons sergeant of an Operational Detachment Alpha, my job was to know mortars, mini-guns, and all other weapon systems in our arsenal.

Each specialty plays a critical role in mission success. I had to teach Afghanistan Special Forces how to shoot, move, and communicate so they no longer needed us.

That was our purpose; we trained other militaries how to conduct warfare so they could operate independently. Personally, my purpose was less about training Afghan Special Forces and more about making sure I was competent and trained enough to keep teammates alive. We all desired to be good at the basics and hunting people and defending ourselves to keep each other safe. We all had a very real fear that none of us ever talked about. We were all terrified to have to look into the lifeless eyes of any teammates. We just wanted to deploy together, do our jobs, and come home together, but not all of the teams on that deployment would get to experience coming home together.

Finally, our first mission came and we were headed to a known enemy valley. Pulling into the valley, it was eerily quiet. It was a long corridor, and the farther you got into it, the higher and closer the mountains got. Finally, we could see the end, and like a cul-de-sac, the valley just came to a stop. It was a horrible position; tall mountains were all around us and we were sitting right in the middle. The only cover was our trucks. However, up until that point, it was completely quiet, and we could see some military-aged males walking around the buildings but no women or children. The majority of the houses were bunched up at the end of the turnaround, and there was only one way in and one way out.

We knew there was heavy enemy presence in this small village. Our plan was to look for weapon caches and mortars. We were fairly certain that a lot of indirect attacks were coming from this location and wanted to find their supplies. As we dismounted the trucks to start our foot patrol through the village, I could see what looked like a white flag waving near a house about half a mile away. I squinted to confirm what I thought might be a white ISIS flag, and suddenly it was game on. Rounds started flying and gunfire started lighting up all around us. Our infantry buddies were driving the trucks; they moved them to a small perimeter so my teammate and I had some cover.

First, we saw muzzle flash from the east and returning fire. Then it lit up from the west, then the north. Before I knew it, my teammate, our Explosive Ordnance Disposal (EOD) Technician, Travis, one of the bravest dudes I have ever met, and I were returning fire in three directions at the same time. This was it. It was happening! I was finally in a two-way range and I loved it. Everything inside me felt like it was coming alive. I had endorphins kicking in that I didn't even know existed. I was overconfident and felt like we were untouchable.

Just then, I could see one of our interpreters attempting to shoot at the houses where I originally saw the white flag. I could see him pulling the trigger, but nothing was happening. He was just frozen, repeatedly pulling the trigger. I couldn't tell if he thought he was shooting back or if he was just panicking, but he had never charged his AK-47 before. He had never put a round in the chamber the entire mission, and now he was exposed, shooting imaginary rounds at a guy who was a pretty damn good shot. I moved the interpreter out of the way and started sending rounds to get the dude's head down. These gunfights were tricky because the guys we were fighting lived there—they had built-in fighting positions, and we were trying to shoot their muzzle flashes. Our Apache helicopter was circling above and couldn't find a single person to light up. We were in the thick of it, and our most effective aerial weapon was rendered useless.

Just as I had moved the interpreter to what I thought was behind cover, time slowed down and I could see bullets slapping the ground and kicking up dirt. Each round that hit moved closer and closer. It was only then that I realized I had not moved the interpreter behind cover; I just got in front of him to return fire. It was only fractions of a second, but to me, it seemed like minutes of watching these rounds head toward me. Just as the rounds finally made it to where I was, I hear a loud screeching yell from what sounded like a prepubescent teenager. It was the interpreter yelling, "AH…BUCK!…THEY SHOT ME!" I started laughing immediately and looked at his leg, which had a hole right through the top. I knew he was going to be okay, but he just stood there staring at me like I had a magic bullet-hole fixer in my pocket.

After laughing for a couple of seconds, I told him to get his ass in the truck on the count of three. I loaded a fresh mag, counted to three, stood up, and dumped the mag on the last spot. I saw muzzle flash. I followed the interpreter inside the vehicle and started patching his leg. He had a through and through, but I could not find the exit wound. I did multiple sweeps and decided to patch the top hole. Once I had finished, I could see blood soaking into the seat of the vehicle. The bullet had traveled up his leg before exiting. I needed to use my gunner's med kit to wrap the second wound. It wasn't a pretty fix, but he was going to be okay. My team sergeant decided to give him a fentanyl lollipop for the drive home. It turned the poor dude green and he started puking all over the damn truck.

After that, I figured it was time to go. I just had the time of my life—I got to patch a bullet wound, and we were surrounded. In my opinion, it was time to pull out of small-arms range and attack with large weapons, or just bounce and call it a day, but my team sergeant had other plans. He figured the location wasn't just a prime ambush spot that we were baited into. He figured they were pro-tecting something important inside those huts. He called out for my teammate and I to get our commandos and clear those huts. Sure, we said, except there was one hiccup with that plan—our commandos were GONE!

It was our first gunfight and all of our commandos hid or ran away. I didn't realize it until that moment, but the twelve to fifteen "highly trained" commandos had left us high and dry. My teammate and I looked outside the trucks and could spot two of them huddled in a safe spot, smoking cigarettes. We informed our team sergeant that we had no commandos, and he replied for us to get our shit together and go find them. This is where I started to notice that he was making poor decisions and our input was not going to be taken on this deployment. But an order was an order.

We jumped out while still taking fire and ran around yelling at the commandos to get up and join us. They just pretended not to understand us and stayed right the fuck where they were. My teammate and I looked at each other and knew our team sergeant wasn't going to let this go. So we said fuck it; we took the one commando who would follow us and started clearing the huts ourselves. We started to get deep into the little village and realized that we were putting ourselves in a really bad spot. We couldn't direct cover into this little maze of buildings, and our only cover were these commandos who were as helpful as the twerp who forgot to load his shit. We finally said fuck it and headed back to the trucks. We called out buildings clear and finally got the approval to push out of this obvious ambush sight. As we started to push out, ambush number two started and rocket-propelled grenades started flying all around us. We found out quickly that the enemy loved to let us roam in quietly, then unleash hell on the way out.

As violent as it was, that trip meant the world to me. I finally got the chance to see if I would freeze in a firefight or keep my head about me and do what I was trained to do. We got lucky on that mission. We got lucky that the enemy didn't maneuver on us, and we got lucky that most of their rounds missed. We got lucky the rocket-propelled grenades were inaccurate and didn't take a direct hit to one of the vehicles, leaving us unable to push out of the kill zone.

ODA 0226 "GFY"

I SOON FOUND OUT THAT IF YOU PLAY WAR FOR LONG enough, the chaos starts to catch up to you. With our confidence high, we went from a single team valley clearance operation into a large-scale battle with ISIS. According to the intelligence, we were heading for our deaths. Every day, new reports of enemy positions were released; thousands of enemy fighters were supposedly on deck waiting for our arrival. By the time we were set to push out, intelligence made it sound like we were going to war with Russia.

The night before the battle, the team was prepping their equipment nervously. It was how we coped with the building anxiety. Go over your equipment, then do it again. Make sure everything was exactly the way you wanted it. Think through as many contingencies as possible and prepare your equipment to deal with those contingencies. The nervous energy was palpable; everyone knew that if intelligence was even slightly inaccurate, we were going to have a fight on our hands that had the potential to go south quickly. In those moments, you block out the thought of your family, and you force yourself to ignore the possibility that you'll never see them again. There is no room for those thoughts. The best chance you have of seeing them again is to prepare mentally and physically for what's to come.

Looking back, no matter how bad the report about the pending fight, I remember looking around that room and seeing guys who filled me with confidence. The bond that was developed from training and combat was solid, and if we were going to do this, we wanted to do it together. Those moments made me feel like my childhood was all meant for this—like I was being prepared to handle high levels of stress and anxiety. It was as though I had been training from a young age to be in that room with those men.

The army taught me how to shoot, move, and communicate, but my mother taught me how to push through stress. She taught me how to endure and see the path from a different perspective. She taught me how to get up after being knocked down. She showed me the depths a person can reach if they never take responsibility for their actions and allow themselves to be victims. Through her life, I learned that it is our responsibility to achieve the goals we want. Nobody can save you from yourself; nobody will feel sorry for you and pull you out from the bottom. No amount of charity will change your state of mind. At some point, we must accept that our paths are ours to choose. If you are walking a path you hate, it is nobody's fault but your own.

Sitting in that room with those men and getting ready for war, I knew that I had chosen the right path for me. I knew that God was planning this day all along. The next four days of combat would change me in a way that I will forever be grateful for. War put me face-to-face with all of the things I endured; it made me see the benefit of being broken. It allowed me to see the strength and callous that I had unknowingly developed as a child. The chaos of war was somehow narrating my life and struggles, as though it was demonstrating life itself.

Throughout my time in the military, I've learned that you can plan for the best outcome possible, but it will inevitably change. All you can do is drive on with your next goal in mind. You will make mistakes, and those around you will save you. Others will make mistakes, and you will come to their aid. We all just do our best in that moment, but at the end of the day, controlling chaos is an impossible task. You have to accept the good with the bad, or the bad will impede your progress. Day one of the battle shoved this lesson down my throat in a way that haunts me to this day. In preparation, I knew that a 320 grenade launcher would be ideal because of the versatility of the rounds. I decided to carry a bandolier around my waist with HE (high-explosive), HEDP (high-explosive dual-purpose), and gas rounds.

There were no great ways to attach the 320 to my kit, so I made an attachment. I ran some 550 cord through the trigger guard and clipped it to my kit. One of my teammates suggested that going through the trigger guard was not the best idea. I agreed, but I assured him it would not be loaded and on safe until I was going to use it. Unfortunately, I was about to learn the hard way that war has a way of changing your plans.

Within minutes of arriving to the valley, we started receiving small-arms fire. Instead of moving and being quick on our feet, the good idea fairy kicked in and someone decided we should put a fifty-caliber machine gun on a rooftop for suppressive fire. My teammate and I were instantly bogged down with a fifty cal, tripod, ammunition, and spare barrels running across open fields while taking fire. The commandos thought the idea was as stupid as we did, so they refused to carry any part of the equipment.

We linked up with a few American soldiers in civilian attire who had apparently been staying in the enemy-occupied valley for days before our arrival. To this day,

I can only guess what agency they worked for, but these guys were no joke. Their leader had hair down to his shoulders and was wearing a nine-millimeter-rated soft vest. He looked like a hippy college professor. His team helped us grab some of the ammo cans and said there is only one location where this fifty cal might serve a purpose. We ran to the building and on the way heard small-arms fire from a close distance. I stopped and loaded my 320 with plans of sending it at the shooter a couple buildings over. Just then, they decided to get to the building and return fire from the high ground.

Still loaded, I put the 320 on safe and reattached it to my side. By this time, I had an AT-4 hanging from my neck, along with my rifle, all while carrying the stupid fucking fifty cal. Once we were inside the building, we started to make our way to the highest rooftop. The college professor went first and climbed a small pole that was leaned up against the wall. He then held down his hand to help pull me up with all my equipment. His buddy was standing below in case I fell. Just then, I could hear a pop and could see smoke coming from the end of my 320. The 320 was sliding up against the wall and slid off safe and pulled the cord that I used to attach it. The round went off and nearly hit me in the leg; it also came close to the guy standing below me.

Once at the top, the professor calmly said, "Your gun went off," then went back to work. I sat there devastated as to how stupid I was for attaching it that way. My leg started to shake uncontrollably. I couldn't tell if it was from the concussion of the round leaving the chamber or my nerves. I sat there for a couple of seconds thinking about all of the things that could have happened: the guy below me getting hit, the round exploding and killing us both, my leg getting shot off. I was in my head, and I had failed on such a huge level that I felt like I didn't belong there. I started to get sick to my stomach when the rounds started flying again, but there was no time to fall apart. War is merciless, and it didn't care that I wasn't in the right frame of mind to keep fighting. It didn't care if I was ready.

It was time to push past the mistake and drive on. We fought in that valley for days, shooting and pushing forward. At night, we would try and sleep for a couple of hours pulling watch shifts. The enemy didn't like to move at night because they knew the aircraft could easily spot them. The ones who did were picked off throughout the night. We were so exhausted that we would doze off while the aircraft sent rounds all night long. The ground shook as the rounds pounded the ground, taking souls. The next morning, we would push off first thing and start the gunfights all over.

As we pushed forward, bodies started appearing along the route. I'll never forget finding the first body, then hearing a teammate yell, "Got one over here!" followed by, "Got another one!" Bodies were littered all over the place, some with 5.56 rounds in them, others peppered with 30 millimeter or 120 millimeter rounds. The 120 millimeter left giant holes in the floor and often caused bodily fluid to leak from the ears and noses of the corpses.

We were starting to find our rhythm, each one of us engaged in separate gunfights simultaneously. During the last day, we were set to push up nearly to the end of the valley. At that point, Rangers would infill on the high ground for over watch and artillery support, then we would link up with our sister team to finish the operation—except that night, our sister team never showed, and our team sergeant pulled us aside and informed us that they weren't coming. One of their guys was a sniper and chasing down an ISIS fighter; he found a good sniper position and slid into place in order to put a round in the fighter's skull. Unfortunately, that position was booby-trapped and he didn't make it.

That night, I didn't sleep at all. I sat in the M-ATV, an armored military vehicle, knowing we were surrounded, and all I could think about was the loss of a fellow Green Beret. The Rangers for whatever reason never made it to their position either. We were in bad shape, with the M-ATVs extremely low on fuel and a supply run becoming increasingly dangerous. The decision finally came that we were not going to push ahead and that we would head out the next morning.

Our EOD Tech was finding improvised explosive devices all the way out of the valley. Every time he dug one up on the way in, someone would replant it right behind us. While leaving the valley, I saw our sister team sergeant staring off into space and I could tell that he was devastated. He was chain-smoking and just staring at the dirt as we drove past. My heart broke to see his pain. That team suffered a huge loss that day, and for the first time, I was seeing how real this all was. Up until that point, we went out and killed the enemy, but that day we took a huge loss, and the severity of what we had been doing finally set in.

DEALING WITH LOSS

—

GROWING UP, ONE OF MY BEST FRIENDS WAS WALKING down the street and was hit by a semitruck. Some people think he walked in front of it, but nobody knows for sure. Then years later, another one of my best friends was hanging out with my brother, and on the way home, he was hit by a drunk driver and killed instantly. My brother peeled his face off the ground, trying to save his life. These things happen to us in life and shake us to our core, changing the structure of our DNA. These moments are difficult to overcome and leave a lingering pain that never entirely disappears. But the loss is still part of our story. It is still something that adds to our strength and character. No loss is ever in vain; it is just up to us to face it and feel the impact.

The losses I experienced when I was young prepared me for all that I would face in the military.

That deployment would bring a lot more gunfights and also bring out the worst in our leadership. Things started to change with our team sergeant; he became increasingly reclusive and started to make more and more dangerous decisions for no apparent reason. During one operation, the aircraft relayed it had two enemy fighters bed down in a compound only a kilometer off our route. Instead of asking the bird to light them up if they maneuver on our position and continue to the objective, my team sergeant grabbed me and a couple of commandos to go find them ourselves. But to no one's surprise, we were having trouble finding commandos again, but we decided to go anyway.

As I looked around, I could see the fear in these commandos' eyes; I knew they were not going to perform well in a close-quarter gunfight. Just then, Travis, our EOD Tech, was jumping out of the armored truck and chasing us down. Even though he was not a Green Beret, he chose to jump into the stack. He was trained to find bombs, not conduct close quarter battle in a stack, but he did not care. He knew we were getting into the shit and wasn't going to let us go alone. I thought, "Thank God, someone I can trust."

We got to the compound, and the team sergeant started to pie the door when he observed one of the fighters and opened fire. The fighters started shooting back, and we were in a point-blank-range gunfight. The AK-47 rounds hitting the wall to our backs sounded like little explosions and shook through the floor. We pulled back to have aircraft hit the dudes with 30 millimeters. The aircraft told us to move back; we were too close. We responded that it wasn't going to happen and to send it now! They lit the compound up with two strafing runs. The rounds impacted so close to us that they made the ground shake. We thought the guys were dead for sure.

We approached the same location, and I watched a commando start to enter the compound and take a round to the forehead. He dropped straight to his back, and I thought, "Well, he's dead." Just then, he jumped up, looked around in complete fear and shock, and got in the back of the stack. We pulled back again, this time taking rounds near our feet as we were running back to our covered position for another strike. The aircraft ended up taking care of the guys, but we almost got killed for two guys who would have been easy targets the minute they left that compound. The delay in our little escapade caused us to miss the target location in time, and we had to turn around, essentially failing our mission.

After that, things got weird on our base. Tensions became extremely high between the team and the team sergeant. Once again, I felt trapped by someone who was not all there mentally. I started to feel like I was back at home as a teenager living with my crazy mother. I hated every day of dealing with this guy and I was not going to stay and be forced to work for him. My decision was made and I was moving on. Little did I know, I was about to face a new type of fight.

FROM ONE FIGHT TO ANOTHER

—

My CHILDHOOD GAVE ME THE STRENGTH TO BECOME A Green Beret, and it gave me the desire to face my fears and see what kind of man I really was. Now, coming home, the real fight was about to begin. I had gotten what I wanted and experienced war and all of the highs and lows it had to offer. Now it was time to see how the experiences were going to affect me. This was going to be a huge challenge because I would be leaving the cover of my friends and teammates.

Soldiers often fail to realize that the things they struggle with are not normal. They fail to realize this because the people they spend the most time with have the same issues they do. Go into a team room of Navy

SEALs, Green Berets, or Rangers, and they will all have similar experiences. None of them will be surprised that you wake up in the middle of the night, and none of them will bat an eye when you stare into space thinking about the friends you have lost. None of them will think twice when you mention the struggles you have with your spouse regarding connecting and being emotionally available. In those environments, PTSD is absolutely normal—it is so normal that we have trouble recognizing the signs and symptoms. Then when we get out of the military, we struggle to deal with civilians because they don't understand us. They can't understand why you get so disrespected while driving or why you have trouble being treated like the new guy at work.

I had gone through too much in my life to allow my experiences to dictate my future. I had to think about my wife and my daughter, and the last thing I wanted to do was to force them to deal with my issues. I had to figure out how to come to terms with my childhood and the experiences I had overseas. This journey wasn't done when I got out of the military. I joined law enforcement because I knew that this was the type of work I was good at, but I had to figure out how to use my history to achieve more. I didn't just want to be okay; I wanted to thrive in life. I wanted to be happy and achieve levels of success that I never thought possible. I started life with a clear path to failure, and I wanted to use that to prove to my daughter that we make our own way no matter what. If you want to live in a big house and drive nice cars, then figure out how and make it happen.

I was going to learn to tame my dragon and use him to burn down every obstacle that would get in my way. I was ready to become better than I ever imagined. I started focusing on my past and talking about it more often. I stopped pretending that my past never happened and started to make peace with it. Before long, it started becoming a source of pride for me. I slowly started becoming proud of the man I had become, considering where I had started.

It is easy to compare yourself to other people and never feel good enough. But none of us start at the same place in life. We all had different experiences that molded us in different ways. The important thing is to know the power that comes from pain. I have achieved what I consider to be a great deal in life because I learned this lesson. I learned that I could increase success and decrease self-sabotage by understanding who I am and why I am that way. Since that realization, I have not only strived to achieve more, but those achievements actually fulfill me. Just obtaining things or achieving goals because you think it will make you appear more impressive or successful does not bring satisfaction. That is what I tried to do through my degrees, ultra-marathons, and various positions. In reality, what I truly wanted was to be a man my family would be proud of.

I never want my daughter to need anything that I can't already provide, but I want to do more than that. What if I can give *her* kids a platform to start their lives from a better place than I did? As Proverbs 13:22 says, "A good man leaves an inheritance to his children's children."

Now I need to map out that structure to help those who grew up like me or who struggle with PTSD. There is a roadmap here that we can all use to find our definition of success. My brother still struggles with our past and has yet to learn to harness its power. I hope this book helps him to realize his true potential and strive to make peace with his pain. I hope to see him riding his dragon one day burning down all obstacles that stand in his way, using his pain as a weapon to carve out the life that makes him truly happy.

To this day, I struggle with PTSD and try to figure out the balance between success and obsession. I struggle to stop every once in a while and appreciate the abundance of gifts and blessings God has given me. When you have a breakthrough and realize you are capable of nearly anything you could think of, it becomes a challenge to hone all of that in. It becomes a challenge to determine exactly what you want. When you awaken to the idea that we are capable of far more than we could ever imagine, then the struggle becomes determining what is truly important to you.

Becoming a pilot or obtaining an advanced degree may be impressive, but will those things bring value to your life? Will those things bring you closer to your goals? What are *your* life goals? The limitless power of our minds becomes a daunting experience of constantly reevaluating life's prospects.

When my ex-wife cheated on me, I was at a crossroads: choose to rise above it and become a better man, or allow it to break me and prove she made the right decision. That choice started me down a path of self-exploration and challenges I needed to face to better understand who I was and what I was capable of. Once I figured out my mind was a powerful tool, I was able to harness it for military successes. I walked away from the military with the question: what could I really accomplish? What are we all truly capable of? My idea of Special Operations changed from combat to entrepreneurship, and then I wondered if I could create wealth past just obtaining a paycheck.

A friend recently asked me what my dragon looks like now and what my current struggles are. It took me a while to answer. At first, I answered with what was bothering me at my job, but I soon realized that a job is only a small part of the equation. A job should provide you with fulfillment and you should enjoy what you do, but at the end of the day, it is still just a job. Your life needs balance, and in order to have balance, you need to know your own heart. My heart struggles to accept that I am a successful man—I have a hard time looking in the mirror and being proud of how far I have come. I always search for the next thing, hoping the next achievement will make me feel successful.

The journey of writing this book has helped me realize that my path has been challenging. The road traveled was not easy, and therefore my success cannot be compared to that of others. I will continue to strive for greater achievements; however, I can now also accept that I have achieved a great deal. Being a good man and a good father are the most important things a man can strive for.

If you struggle with your past, then there is good news. You just read the way that I started to tame my dragon and face my past. For me, this book is the key. Now, I am not saying that to focus on your past you have to write a book, but I am saying that you need to put pen to paper and start from the beginning. When moments jump out at you as significant, write them down. Don't evaluate them initially; just get them on paper.

The journey through your past will reveal long-lost secrets and start to connect dots. Create the timeline and start to evaluate the moments that really affected your life. How are those moments affecting you now? How are the good and bad decisions connected to those pinnacle moments in your history? These are all questions you should ask once it's time to dig deeper. Soon you will paint the picture of your existence. This is a powerful thing to do; you're getting to know yourself.

Once you know yourself, you become a very powerful being. It is then that you can look your dragon in the face and understand it. Once it is understood, it is no longer a force of destruction but a powerful tool. When it is understood and treated with respect, it will be time to mount your dragon and burn your goals to the fucking ground. Nothing will stop you; anything you want will be obtainable. The obstacles that once felt like they were insurmountable will be minor pains in the ass for you. You will be self-aware and confident in your abilities. You will recognize strength from weakness and know when something is right for you and when it is time to go.

My self-awareness has recently led me to end my law enforcement career. The Denver riots were eye-opening for me. The riots were a result of the death of a black male in Minneapolis after being detained by police. The riots caused absolute chaos in Denver, Colorado. People throwing rocks and Molotov cocktails at us while we stood vulnerable on the side of rapid deployment vehicles. These vehicles were trucks with standing platforms attached to the outside so officers can quickly jump off and deploy less-lethal munitions. We were getting radio updates that fellow officers were being targeted and struck by vehicles while standing on the trucks. Two officers were severely injured from the vehicle attack. I was nearly struck by a vehicle after it smashed into two other parked cars and was headed for myself and a group of officers. I pulled my firearm and knew I had to protect the officers. I was sighted in on a driver as he jumped the curb and headed toward us. Just then, he looked at me and cranked the wheel, getting back onto the street and speeding off.

We were dealt with instances like this for fifteen hours straight for days on end. These scenarios were taking me back, and I felt at home in the chaos. But I had no idea that the department would soon turn on us. Shortly after the riots, politics set in and department heads caved. They allowed everyone to treat us like the bad guys knowing we just gave them everything we had and risked it all for days.

I knew myself well enough to know it was time to move on. My self-awareness gave me confidence that I was not meant to deal with the challenges law enforcement was about to face. I was not the right person for the job anymore. This awareness likely saved my family and me a lot of pain and heartache. I would have never made that decision if I did not spend the time getting to know myself. I would have fallen in line like so many others, and I would have been destroyed when I clashed with my changing environment.

I hope this book inspires you to put pen to paper and

start the journey of self-awareness. It is only then that you will truly chase what is meaningful to you in this blessing of a life.

I would like to end this book by saying thank you for taking the time to read it. I hope my story can start you down a path of accepting your past and using it to create goodness in your life. We are all broken and have all done things that we are not proud of. None of us are perfect, and our greatest attribute is our willingness to keep pushing forward.

Never allow your past to create roadblocks for your future. We all have an obligation to provide for future generations, to leave this world better than when we were born into it. Wake up every morning and work harder than anyone else around you; you owe it to yourself and your family to be better than anyone expects you to be. The more pain you endured throughout your life, the larger and fiercer your dragon. Face it, tame it, and then ride it to the destination of your dreams. When trained, it will burn down every obstacle in your way, as it is your most powerful tool. God bless and good luck.

ABOUT THE AUTHOR

—

SEAN "BUCK" ROGERS is a former Green Beret and law enforcement officer.

Born in Phelan, California, Buck refused to allow his childhood trauma to shape his future and utilized his past to obtain fulfillment in life. He quickly learned that to survive life in the desert, you must be ruthless and fight for what you need.

Trapped in an abusive and neglecting home, he quickly learned he needed to strive for something better. At the age of sixteen, Buck was able to escape from home and landed in New York where his journey began. Holding many jobs and living life on his own made him grow as a young man until he started his military career. There was never a moment where he doubted he could make it. Buck's impulsive, relentless behavior shaped him to achieve more than he ever imagined.

After joining the military, he always strived for more. Buck went to Ranger selection, and despite getting hurt in the course, it taught him many lessons he later used for Special Forces Selection and earned his Green Beret. Buck continued to hone his mental toughness through running and education; having run multiple ultramarathons and earning a master's degree, Buck continues to strive for greatness. He finished his career serving the Denver Police Department and is constantly helping others through his YouTube channel *FNG Academy* and podcast *The FNG Podcast*.